Stitch by Stitch

Volume 9

TORSTAR BOOKS

NEW YORK · TORONTO

TORSTAR BOOKS INC.
580 WHITE PLAINS ROAD
TARRYTOWN, NEW YORK 10591

Knitting and crochet abbreviations

approx = approximately	in = inch(es)	sl st = slip stitch
beg = begin(ning)	inc = increase(e)(ing)	sp = space(s)
ch = chain(s)	K = knit	st(s) = stitch(es)
cm = centimeter(s)	oz = ounce(s)	tbl = through back of
cont = continue(ing)	P = purl	loop(s)
dc = double crochet	patt = pattern	tog = together
dec = decrease(e)(ing)	psso = pass slipped	tr = triple crochet
dtr = double triple	stitch over	WS = wrong side
foll = follow(ing)	rem = remain(ing)	wyib = with yarn in
g = gram(s)	rep = repeat	back
grp = group(s)	RS = right side	wyif = with yarn in front
dc = half double	sc = single crochet	yd = yard(s)
crochet	sl = slip	yo = yarn over

A guide to the pattern sizes

		10	12	14	16	18	20
Bust	in	32½	34	36	38	40	42
	cm	83	87	92	97	102	107
Waist	in	25	26½	28	30	32	34
	cm	64	67	71	76	81	87
Hips	in	34½	36	38	40	42	44
	cm	88	92	97	102	107	112

Torstar Books also offers a range of acrylic book stands, designed to keep instructional books such as *Stitch by Stitch* open, flat and upright while leaving the hands free for practical work.

For information write to Torstar Books Inc., 580 White Plains Road, Tarrytown, New York 10591.

Library of Congress Cataloging in Publication Data
Main entry under title:

Stitch by stitch.

Includes index.
1. Needlework. I. Torstar Books (Firm)
TT705.S74 1984   746.4   84-111
ISBN 0-920269-00-1 (set)

987654321

© Marshall Cavendish Limited 1984

Printed in Belgium

Contents

*Working the shell and chain motif
*Making a complete lace fabric
*Working a simple daisy
*Pattern for two centerpiece doilies and two lace motif collars

Working the shell and chain motif

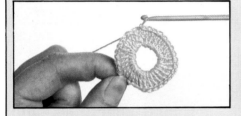

1 Begin by working 10 chains and then join the last chain to the first with a slip stitch in the usual way. Make 3 chains which should be counted as the first double and work 31 doubles all into the center of the ring. Push the doubles together as you work so that they all fit neatly into the ring. Join the last double to the 3rd of the first 3 chains with a slip stitch. Join each round in the same way.

2 Now make 3 chains to count as the first double of the 2nd round. Work a double into the double at the base of these 3 chains. Now work 3 chains followed by 2 doubles into the same place to complete the first V-shaped shell. Make sure that you wind the yarn correctly around the left hand to maintain an even tightness while working with fine cotton.

3 Make 7 chains and skip the next 3 stitches. Now work 2 doubles, 3 chains and 2 doubles all into the next (4th) stitch to complete this shell. Count the stitches carefully when working with fine cotton, since it is quite easy to overlook a stitch worked in a previous round.

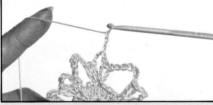

4 Continue to work 7 chains followed by a shell into every following 4th stitch all the way around the circle. Finish the round with 7 chains and join the last chain as before to the beginning of the round. You should have 8 shells with a 7-chain loop linking each shell.

5 Work the next round in same way. Work a slip stitch in center loop of first shell so that you are in the correct position to start working the pattern. When working a larger motif you should slip stitch into each chain or stitch until the correct place has been reached. Now work 3 chains.

6 Complete the shell in the same way as at the beginning of the previous round, working each stitch into this first 3-chain loop in the center of the first shell.

7 Complete the round by working a shell into the center of each shell worked in the previous round with a 7-chain loop between each shell. Join the last chain to the beginning of the round as before.

8 Now slip stitch across to the center of the first 3-chain loop. Work the first shell as before. Now make 4 chains and work a single crochet over the middle of the *two* 7-chain loops, inserting the hook under the first of these loops. Complete the single crochet in the usual way.

9 Now make 4 chains and work a shell as before into the center of the next shell. By drawing the loops together in this way you form the shells worked in this round into points.

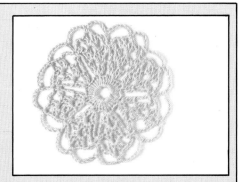

10 Continue all around the motif in the same way, working 4 chains at each side of the center single crochet (holding the loops together) and a shell into each shell all the way around. Join the last chain to the beginning of the round as before.

11 To complete the motif with a chain border, slip stitch to the center of the first shell as before. Now work a single crochet into the same place as the slip stitch followed by 7 chains.

12 Continue to work all around the motif, working a double into each single crochet between the shells and a single crochet into the center of each shell with 7 chains linking each stitch. Join the last chain with a slip stitch as before and fasten off to complete the motif.

Making a complete lace fabric

If you find a pattern for a single motif which you would like to join together with crochet to make a lace fabric for a tablecloth or shawl, it is quite easy to work out your own pattern for joining the motifs together and filling the spaces created when four or more circular motifs are joined in this way.

Here we show you how to join and fill 4 of the shell and chain motifs worked previously with a simple pattern which could be adapted to suit a number of different motifs.

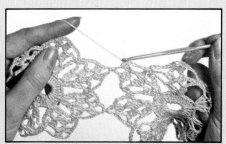

1 Make a shell and chain motif omitting the last chain round. Now work the first 3 rounds of the next motif and the first two doubles of the first shell in the next round. Make 1 chain. Hold the wrong sides of the motifs together and work a single crochet into the corresponding shell in the first motif.

2 Now work 1 chain and complete the shell being worked in the 2nd motif. Continue in pattern to the next shell and join this in the same way as before to the first motif. Now complete the round as before and fasten off the yarn.

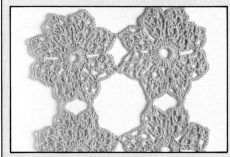

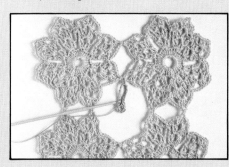

3 Join 2 more motifs in exactly the same way, joining the corresponding shells where necessary. Detailed directions on how to join more than 2 motifs are given in the pattern (see "Collar") on page 8.

4 To work the filling for the center space make 6 chains and join into a circle with a slip stitch. Work 6 chains and with the right side of the lace fabric facing work a single crochet into one of the points where motifs are joined together. Now work 6 more chains and work a single crochet into the center ring. The number of chains worked will vary depending on the size of the space to be filled and the yarn used.

5 Continue to work a double 6-chain loop all the way around to link the motifs and the center ring, working a single crochet into each single crochet linking the 7-chain loops together between the shells and into the point where the motifs are joined each time.

Working a simple daisy

Unlike most motifs this daisy is worked petal by petal, so that each individual petal is completed and the yarn fastened off before the next petal is begun. Since the motif has not been worked in continuous rounds there are no linking chains or stitches worked between each petal, and the flower shape is clearly formed.

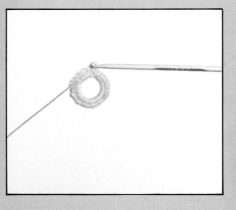

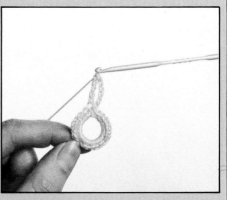

1 Start the daisy with 10 chains joined into a circle with a slip stitch. Make 2 chains and then work 23 single crochets into the circle so that there are 24 stitches in all. Remember to join each round with a slip stitch, linking the last chain or stitch to the top of the chain worked at the beginning of the round.

2 Each stitch in the next round should be worked into the back loop only of the stitches worked in the previous round. Start with 5 chains. Now make 1 chain and then work a triple into the next stitch.

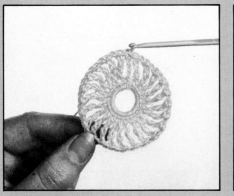

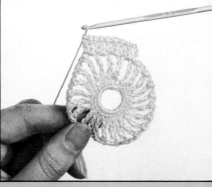

3 Complete the round by working 1 chain and a triple into each stitch all the way around. Finish with 1 chain, slip stitch into 4th of the 5 chains.

4 Start the first petal by making 3 chains followed by a double worked into each space between the stitches and each triple until you have worked 9 doubles in all, including the first 3 chains. These 9 stitches form the base of the first petal.

5 Now turn and complete the petal on these stitches leaving the remaining stitches unworked for the time being. Make 4 chains. Skip the first stitch. Now leaving the last loop of each triple on the hook so that each stitch is incomplete, work a triple into each of the petal stitches. You should have 9 loops on the hook in all.

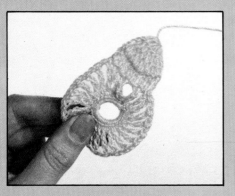

6 Now wind the yarn over the hook and draw it through all the loops on the hook to shape the top of the petal and complete all the triples. Fasten off the yarn to complete the first petal.

7 Rejoin the yarn to the same stitch where the last double of the first petal was worked so that the petals are linked at the base. Now work the next petal in exactly the same way as before.

8 To complete the flower work 4 more petals in exactly the same way, rejoining the yarn to the base of the previous petal each time to link them all together.

Fred Mancini

Centerpiece doilies

Fluted or picot edging gives doilies a touch of elegance.

Doily with fluted edge

Size
Diameter 11in (28cm)

Materials
3 x 100yd (90m) of a medium-weight mercerized crochet cotton for each doily
Size B (2.50mm) crochet hook

Gauge
The first 2 rounds measure 2in (5cm) in diameter.

To make
Make 10ch, join with sl st to first ch.
1st round 3ch to count as first dc, then work 23 dc into circle, sl st to top of 3ch.
2nd round 3ch, *2dc into next dc, rep from * 10 times more, 2dc into next dc, sl st into top of 3ch. 36 sts.
3rd round 3ch, 1dc into next dc, *4ch, skip next 2dc, ldc into each of next 2dc, rep from * 7 times more, 4ch, sl st into top of 3ch. 9 groups of 4ch.
4th round 3ch, 2dc into next dc, *5ch, 1dc into next tr, 2dc into next dc, rep from * 7 times more, 5ch, sl st into top of 3ch.
5th round 3ch, 2dc into next dc, 1dc into next dc, *4ch, 1dc into next dc, 2dc into next dc, 1dc into next dc, rep from * 7 times more, 4ch, sl st into top of 3ch.
6th round 3ch, 2dc into each of next 2dc, 1dc into next dc, *3ch, 1dc into next dc, 2dc into each of next 2dc, 1dc into next dc, rep from * 7 times more, 3ch, sl st into top of 3ch.
7th round 3ch, 2dc into each of next 4dc, 1dc into next dc, *2ch, 1dc into next dc, 2dc into each of next 4dc, 1dc into next dc, rep from * 7 times more, 2ch, sl st into top of 3ch.
8th round 3ch, *2dc into each of next 3dc, 1dc into each of next 2dc, 2dc into each of next 3dc, 1dc into next dc, 1ch, 1dc into next dc, rep from * 8 times more omitting last dc on last rep, sl st into top of 3ch.
9th round *10ch, 1sc between 2 single dc of 16dc group, 10ch, 1sc into next 1ch sp, rep from * 8 times more, sl st into first of 10ch.
10th round sl st to center of first 10ch loop, *10ch, 1sc into center of next 10ch loop, rep from * to end of round omitting last sc on last rep, sl st to first ch.
11th round As 10th round.
12th round sl st to center of first 10ch. loop, *5ch, 1sc into next 10ch loop, 5ch, 1sc into same 10ch loop, rep from * to end, omitting last sc on last rep,

sl st to first ch.
13th round 4ch to count as first tr, work 14tr, into first 5ch loop, *15tr into next 5ch loop, rep from * to end, sl st to top of 4ch.
14th round 4ch, work 1tr into each tr all around, sl st into top of 4ch.
15th round 4ch, skip first st, *sl st into next st, 1sc into next st, 4ch, rep from * all around, sl st into first ch. Fasten off.

Doily with picot edging

Size
Diameter 9½in (24cm)

Materials
2 x 100yd (90m) of a medium-weight mercerized crochet cotton for each doily
Size B (2.50mm) crochet hook

Gauge
The first 2 rounds measure 2in (5cm) in diameter.

To make
Work first 8 rounds as for first doily.
9th round 1ch, skip next dc, *(1hdc, 1ch and 1hdc) all into next dc, skip next dc, (1dc, 1ch and 1dc) all into next dc, skip next dc, (1tr, 1ch and 1tr) all into next dc, (1dtr, 1ch and 1tr) all into sp before next dc, skip next dc, (1tr, 1ch and 1tr) all into next dc, skip next dc, (1dc, 1ch and 1dc) all into next dc, skip next dc, (1hdc, 1ch and 1hdc) all into next dc, 1sc into next 1ch sp, skip first 2 dc of next group, rep from * to end, working last sc into last 1ch sp, join with sl st to first ch.
10th round 3ch to count as first dc, (1dc, 2ch and 2dc) into first ch sp, *10ch, 1sc into 1ch sp between dtr group at center, 10ch, (2dc, 2ch and 2dc) —called shell—all into sc between fan shapes, rep from * to last fan shape, 10ch, 1sc into 1ch sp between last dtr group at center, 10ch, join with sl st to top of 3ch.

Kim Sayer

11th round 3ch, (1dc, 2ch and 2dc) into same place as sl st, *8ch, work a shell into next sc between dtr group, 8ch, work a shell into 2ch loop at center of next group, rep from * to end, 8ch, join with sl st to top of 3ch.

12th round Sl st to center of first shell, 3ch to count as first dc, 3ch, sl st into 3rd ch from hook—picot formed—, (1dc, 1 picot) twice into same place as sl st, *4ch, 1dc around center of both 8ch loops, 1 picot, 4ch, (1dc, 1 picot) 3 times into center of next shell, rep from * to end, omitting last picot group, sl st into first picot. Fasten off.

Lacy collars

Brighten up a plain dress with a pretty lace collar.

Cream collar

Size
To fit average neck. Depth, 4¾in (12cm).

Materials
2 x 150yd (140m) of a fine mercerized crochet cotton Nos. 12 and 10 (.75 and 1.00mm) steel hooks

Gauge
One motif is 2¼in (6cm) in diameter.

The motif
Using No. 12 (.75mm) hook, make 10ch, sl st into first ch to form a circle.
1st round 3ch to count as first dc, work 31dc into circle, sl st into top of 3ch.
2nd round 3ch, work (1dc, 3ch and 2dc) all into same place as sl st—starting shell—7ch, * skip next 3dc, work (2dc, 3ch and 2dc) all into next dc—shell formed—, 7ch, rep from * all around, sl st into top of 3ch.
3rd round Sl st into first 3ch sp, 3ch, work a starting shell into same place as sl st, *7ch, work a shell into 3ch sp of next shell, rep from *, ending with 7ch, sl st into top of 3ch.
4th round Sl st into first 3ch sp, 3ch, work a starting shell into same place as sl st, *4ch, 1sc around both 7ch loops, 4ch, 1 shell into 3ch loop of next shell, rep from * all around, ending with 4ch, sl st into top of 3ch.
5th round Sl st to 2nd ch of 3ch sp, 1sc into same place as sl st, 7ch, *1dc into next sc, 7ch, 1sc into center of next shell, 7ch, rep from * all around, ending with 7ch, sl st into first st. Fasten off. Make 13 more motifs in the same way.

Collar
1st row Using No. 10 (1.00mm) hook and with RS facing join yarn to left-hand 7ch loop of one petal with sl st, (7ch, 1sc into next loop) 6 times, *2ch, sl st into

the right-hand loop of one petal of the next motif, (7ch, 1sc into next loop) 5 times, rep from * 12 times, ending with 2ch, 1 tr into 3rd of 7ch. Turn.
2nd row *6ch, 1sc into next 7ch loop, rep from * to end, ending with 2ch, 1 tr into 3rd of 7ch. Turn.
3rd row As 2nd.
4th row 6ch, *1sc into next ch sp, 5ch, rep from * to last sp, 1sc into last ch sp, 2ch, 1 tr into 3rd of 6ch. Turn.
5th and 6th rows As 4th.
7th row 6ch, *1sc into next ch sp, 4ch, rep from * to last sp, 1sc into last sp, 2ch, 1 tr into 3rd of 6ch. Turn.
8th row As 7th.
9th row Work 3sc into each 4ch sp. Turn.
10th row 4ch, *skip next 2sc, work 1hdc into next sc, 2ch, rep from * to end, working last hdc into turning ch. Turn.
11th row Work 3sc into each ch sp. Turn.

12th row 3ch, *skip next sc, 1sc into next sc, rep from * to end. Turn.
13th row *4ch, 1sc into next ch loop, rep from * to end. Turn.
14th row *5ch, 1sc into next ch loop, rep from * to end. Fasten off.

Tie
Using 2 strands of yarn tog make a twisted cord approx. 36in (90cm) long. Thread through row of holes between sc rows. Sew the point of the next 2 free adjacent petals together on each motif.

Yellow collar

Size
To fit average neck. Depth, 4¾in (12cm).

Materials
2 x 150yd (140m) of a fine mercerized crochet cotton No. 10 (1.00mm) crochet hook

Jean Claude Volpeliere

1 snap

Gauge

One motif is 2¼in (6cm) in diameter.

The motif

Using No. 10 (1.00mm) hook make 10ch, sl st into first ch to form a circle.

1st round 2ch to count as first sc, work 23sc into circle, sl st into back loop of first sc.

2nd round 5ch to count as first tr and 1ch, * working into back loop only, work 1 tr into next sc, 1ch, rep from * all around, finishing sl st into 4th of 5ch. Make petals as follows:

1st petal

Next row 3ch to count as 1dc, (1dc into next sp, 1dc into next tr) 4 times. Turn.

Next row 4ch, skip first dc, now leaving last loop of each on hook work 1tr into each st, yo and draw through all

9 loops on hook, 1 ch. Fasten off.

2nd petal

Next row Join yarn to same tr as last dc of first petal, 3ch, (1dc into next sp, 1dc into next tr) 4 times. Turn.
Complete as given for first petal.
Make 4 more petals in the same way, working the last dc into the same sp as first dc of first petal. Fasten off.
Make 11 more motifs.

Collar

Using No. 10 (1.00mm) hook make 221 ch.

Base row 1sc into 2nd ch from hook, 1 sc into each ch to end. Turn.

Next row 2ch to count as first hdc, 1hdc into each st to end. Turn. 220hdc.
Shape as follows:

1st row Sl st over first hdc, work 6ch, 1dc into next hdc, 3ch, 1dc into next hdc, (3ch, skip next hdc, 1dc into next hdc)

3 times, skip next 3hdc, 1dc into next hdc, (3ch, skip next hdc, 1dc into next hdc) 3 times, 3ch, *(1dc, 3ch and 1dc) all into next hdc—V formed—3ch, 1dc into next hdc, (3ch, skip next hdc, 1dc into next hdc) 3 times, skip next hdc, 1dc into next hdc, (3ch, skip next hdc, 1dc into next hdc) 3 times, 3ch, rep from * 10 times more, ending with (1dc, 3ch and 1dc) all into next hdc. Turn. (2hdc unworked).

2nd row 6ch, 1dc into first V, *(3ch, 1dc into next sp) 4 times, 1dc into next sp, (3ch, 1dc into next sp) 3 times, 3ch, work a V into next V, rep from * to end. Turn.
Rep last row twice more.

5th row As 2nd row but work 4ch instead of 3ch throughout.
Rep last row twice more.
Join on motifs as follows:

7th row (WS) 6ch, 1dc into first V, 4ch, 1dc into next sp, 2ch, place flower motif behind collar with RS tog and work 2dc into loop at end of one petal, 2ch, 1dc into next sp on collar, 3ch, 1dc into next sp, 3ch, 1dc into next sp, sl st into loop at top of next petal on motif, 1dc into next ch sp, (3ch, 1dc into next sp) twice, 2ch, 2dc into loop at top of next petal, 2ch, 1dc into next sp, 3ch, *work a V into next V, 4ch, 1dc into next sp, 2ch, place next flower motif behind collar with RS tog and work 2dc into loop at top of one petal, 2ch, 1dc into next sp on collar, (3ch, 1dc into next sp) twice, sl st into loop at top of next petal, 1dc into next sp, (3ch, 1dc into next sp) twice, 2ch, 2dc into loop at top of next petal, 2ch, 1dc into next sp, 3ch, rep from * 10 times more, ending with 4ch, 1dc into next sp, work a V into last V. Turn.

8th row 6ch, 1dc into first V, 3ch, 1dc into next sp, 3ch, 1dc into base of next 2dc, 6ch, (1dc between next 2 petals, 6ch, 1sc into end of petal, 6ch) 3 times, 1dc between next 2 petals, 6ch, 1dc into base of 2dc, 3ch, 1dc into next sp, 3ch, *work a V into next V, 3ch, 1dc into next sp, 3ch, 1dc into base of 2dc, 6ch, (1dc between next 2 petals, 6ch, 1sc into end of petal, 6ch) 3 times, 1dc between next 2 petals, 6ch, 1dc into base of 2dc, 3ch, 1dc into next sp, 3ch, rep from * 10 times more, ending with a V into last V. Turn.

9th row 6ch, 1dc into first V, 4ch, (1sc into 6ch loop, 5ch, 1sc into next dc, 5ch, 1sc into next 6ch loop, 5ch, 1sc into sc at end of petal) 3 times, 5ch, 1sc into 6ch loop, 5ch, 1sc into next dc, 5ch, 1sc into next 6ch loop, 2ch, *1 V into next V, 4ch, (1sc into 6ch loop, 5ch, 1sc into next dc, 5ch, 1sc into next 6ch loop, 5ch, 1sc into sc at end of petal) 3 times, 5ch, 1sc into 6ch loop, 2ch, rep from * 10 times more, ending with 4ch, a V into last V. Fasten off.
Sew on snap.

* Jacquard patterns in crochet
* Working with several colors
* Working the diamond pattern
* Diamond pattern variation
* Pattern for a Jacquard crib blanket

Jacquard patterns in crochet

Jacquard is the name used to describe heavily patterned fabrics with complex designs, which are used for upholstery and drapery materials, brocades, carpets and some knitting and crochet patterns. The patterns originate from the turn of the nineteenth century when a Frenchman, Joseph Jacquard, invented a mechanical device which, when it was attached to a loom, enabled the weaver to create far more complex and colorful patterns than had hitherto been possible.

Although patterns worked in crochet cannot be so intricate as those woven into a cloth fabric, you can still create a variety of colorful patterns using different shapes or motifs in two or more colors to create the Jacquard effect.

The patterns can be worked in a variety of yarns, although you will find that the best results are obtained when a medium-weight yarn such as knitting worsted is used, since this creates a firm, even fabric. Clear colors help to maintain the

definition in the design, although subtle shades could be used to create a pattern similar in appearance to those worked in Fair Isle knitting.

The fabric should be worked in one of the shallow crochet stitches—single crochet or half doubles, for example—so that you obtain as clear an outline as possible. You will lose definition if you try to work in a double or triple crochet fabric, however clear and bright the colors you are using might be.

Working with several colors

It is very important to maintain an even stitch gauge when working Jacquard patterns, since it is quite easy to pull the yarn too tight when it is being stranded across the back of the work, thus distorting the fabric on the right side.

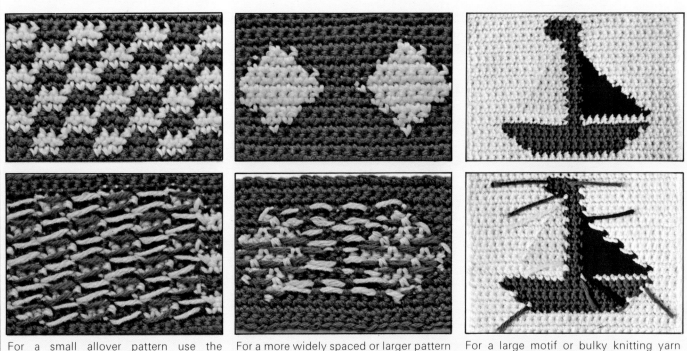

For a small allover pattern use the stranding method to carry the yarn not in use across the back of the fabric (see Crochet course 8, Volume 2, page 16).

For a more widely spaced or larger pattern use the weaving method when carrying the yarn across the back of the work (see Crochet course 8, Volume 2, page 17).

For a large motif or bulky knitting yarn use separate balls of yarn for each color as shown here (see Crochet course 9, Volume 2, page 20).

Fred Mancini

Working the diamond pattern

Here we show you how to work a simple pattern in two colors, using diamond shapes to create the pattern. By repeating the diamonds several times across the row you can create a simple Jacquard effect. Once you have practiced working this sample you should be able to work any of the patterned squares featured in the crib blanket on page 13.

Use knitting worsted and a size G (4.5mm) hook to make a sample like the one shown here and work each row in single crochet. To repeat the pattern several times add an extra 9 chains for each additional diamond, plus 3 extra chains for the 3 stitches worked between each diamond shape.

So that the directions are easy to follow, each color is represented by a letter, in this case A for the main color and B for the contrasting color.

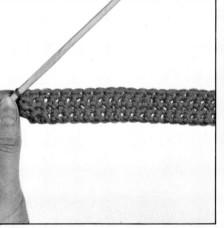

1 Begin the sample by making 28 chains and working 4 rows in A, with 27 single crochet in each row. Remember to start the first row by working into the 3rd chain from the hook.

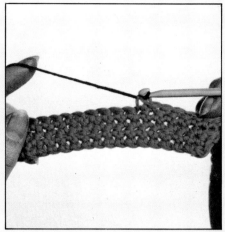

2 Now begin to work the diamond pattern by working 7 stitches in A, including the turning chain. Change to B on the 7th of these stitches, drawing the yarn through the last 2 loops of the last stitch to complete it (refer to Crochet course 8).

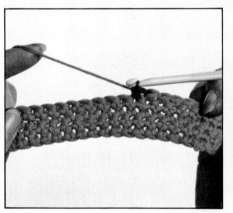

3 Now work 1 stitch in B, holding A at back of work and drawing A through the last two loops of this stitch to complete it and change yarns once more. If necessary make sure the new yarn is secure by pulling it firmly from behind.

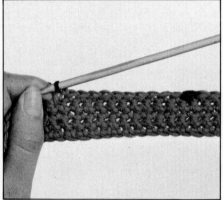

4 Now work 11 stitches in A, weaving B across the back of the fabric in the correct way. Change to B while working the last stitch in A as before.

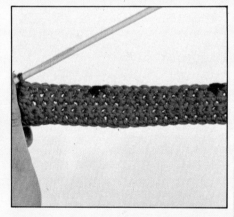

5 Now complete the row by working 1 more stitch in B and working to the end of the row in A. There is no need to carry B to the edge of the fabric as the sides are worked in A only.

6 Now turn and work 5 stitches in A. Do not forget to count the turning chain as one stitch. The WS of the fabric is now facing so the extra yarn will be woven into the side facing you.

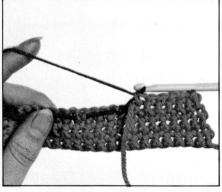

7 Work the next stitch in A, changing to B while completing the stitch by taking B to the back of the work (RS) and bringing A to the front of the work (WS).

8 Now work 3 stitches in B, changing to A on the last stitch as before by bringing B to the front and taking A to the back (RS) of the fabric.

continued

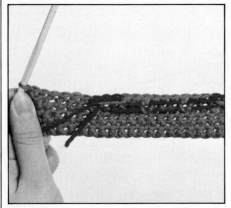

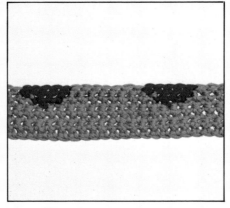

9 Complete the row by working 9 more stitches in A, 3 in B and 6 in A, changing color as before on the last stitch worked in each color.

10 Now turn and continue to work next row in diamond pattern as set, working 5 stitches in B in each diamond, working 1 less stitch in A each time.

11 Work the next row in the same way, but working 7 stitches in each diamond and 1 stitch less in A each time.

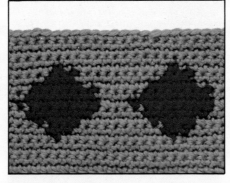

12 Complete the widest part of the diamond on the next row by working 9 stitches in each diamond and 1 less stitch in A each time, with only 3 stitches in A between each diamond and at each end of the row.

13 Complete the diamond by working the rows in reverse, so that you will work 7, 5, 3 and finally one stitch in B and working extra stitches in A on every row.

14 Here we show you the WS of the sample with all the extra yarn woven neatly into the back of the fabric.

Diamond pattern variation

It is quite simple to work a variation on the same diamond pattern, alternating the position of the diamonds to create a much more complex design which could be used as an allover pattern for a sweater.

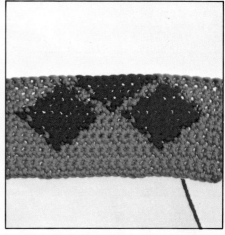

1 Work the first 9 rows of the diamond pattern as before, then begin to work another diamond on the next row in the center of the fabric by working 1 stitch in B into the 2nd of the 3 stitches worked between the diamonds.

2 Turn and continue to work in pattern as before but working the central diamond at the same time as the 2 outer motifs until these have been completed and the first 5 rows of the central diamond have been worked.

Fred Mancini

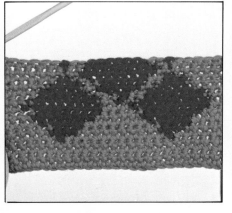

Fred Mancini

3 Now begin to work the 2 outer diamonds on the next row so that you start the row by working 7 stitches in A, 1 in B, 2 in A and then 7 in B across the central diamond.

4 Complete the row by working 2 stitches in A followed by 1 in B and then completing the row in A. Thus the two outer diamonds are worked directly over those already completed.

5 Now work all 3 diamonds at the same time until the central diamond has been completed, then complete the 2 outer diamonds, working in A only at the center. To work a fabric entirely in diamonds work alternate diamonds in this way leaving 1 row between each diamond and starting the next one directly above it.

Bundle of joy

For a cozy quilted crib blanket, we have worked a Jacquard front and solid back and put a layer of batting in between.

Size
35in (89cm) long by 25½in (65cm) wide.

Materials
9 x 2oz (40g) balls of a knitting worsted in main color (A)
4 balls in each of 2 contrasting colors (B and C)
Sizes E and F (3.50 and 4.00mm) crochet hooks
3½yd (3m) of synthetic batting 36in (90cm) wide

Gauge
One motif measures 5½in (14cm) by 4¾in (12cm).

Note The stitch used throughout is sc. When changing color in the middle of a row it must be remembered that the change of color is effected on the last stage of the last st worked before the change of color: in first color insert hook into next st and draw yarn through, as if to make a sc, drop the color being used and draw through 2nd color, so that the 2nd color is now ready to be used for the next st.

Back
Plain motif (make 30)
Using size F (4.00mm) hook and A, make 24ch.

Base row 1sc into 2nd ch from hook, 1sc into each ch to end. Turn.
Patt row 1ch to count as first sc, 1sc into each sc to end. Turn.
Rep patt row 27 times. Fasten off.

Motif 1 (make 12)
Using size F (4.00mm) hook and B, make 25ch.
1st row Working first st into 2nd ch from hook and 1sc into each ch, work 2 A, 2 C, 16 B, 2 C, 2A. Turn.
2nd row 1ch, 3 A, 2 C, 14 B, 2 C, 3A. Turn.
3rd row 1ch, 1 C, 3 A, 2 C, 12 B, 2 C, 3 A, 1 C. Turn.
4th row 1ch, 2 C, 3 A, 2 C, 10 B, 2 C, 3 A, 2 C. Turn.
5th row 1ch, 1 B, 2 C, 3 A, 2 C, 8 B, 2 C, 3 A, 2 C, 1 B. Turn.
6th row 1ch, 2 B, 2 C, 3 A, 2 C, 6 B, 2 C, 3 A, 2 C, 2 B. Turn.
7th row 1ch, 3 B, 2 C, 3 A, 2 C, 4 B, 2 C, 3 A, 2 C, 3 B. Turn.
8th row 1ch, 4 B, 2 C, 3 A, 2 C, 2 B, 2 C, 3 A, 2 C, 4 B. Turn.
9th row 1ch, 5 B, 2 C, 3 A, 1 C, 2 B, 1 C, 3 A, 2 C, 5 B. Turn.
10th row 1ch, 6B, 2 C, 3 A, 2 C, 3 A, 2 C, 6 B. Turn.
11th row 1ch, 7 B, 2 C, 6 A, 2 C, 7 B. Turn.
12th row 1ch, 9 B, 1 C, 4 A, 1 C, 9 B. Turn.
13th-24th rows Work 12th–1st rows in this order. Fasten off.

Motif 2 (make 6)
Using size F (4.00mm) hook and C, make 25ch.
1st row Working first st into 2nd ch from hook and 1sc into each ch, work with A to end. Turn.

hook and 1sc into each ch, work (4C, 4 B) 3 times. Turn.
2nd row 1ch, (4 B, 4 C) 3 times. Turn.
3rd row 1ch, (4 C, 4 B) 3 times. Turn.
4th row 1ch, (4 B, 4 C) 3 times. Turn.
5th row 1ch, (4 C, 4 B) 3 times. Turn.
6th row 1ch, (4 B, 4 C) 3 times. Turn.
Rep these 6 rows 3 times. Fasten off.

Motif 3 (make 6)
Using size F (4.00mm) hook and B, make 25ch.
1st row Working first st into 2nd ch from hook and 1sc into each ch, work with B to end. Turn.
2nd and 3rd rows Work with B. Turn.
4th row 1ch, 3 C, (2 B, 2 C) 4 times, 2 B, 3 C. Turn.
5th row As 4th.
6th row Work with C. Turn.
7th-12th rows Rep last 6 rows working A instead of B. Now work the last 12 rows once more. Fasten off.

Motif 4 (make 6)
Using size F (4.00mm) hook and A, make 25ch.
1st row Working first st into 2nd ch from hook and 1sc into each ch, work with A to end. Turn.
2nd row Work with A. Turn.
3rd row 1ch, 5 A, 2 B, 4 A, 2 C, 4 A, 2 B, 5 A. Turn.
4th row 1ch, 4 A, 4 B, 2 A, 4 C, 2 A, 4 B, 4 A. Turn.
5th row As 4th.
6th row As 3rd.
7th row 1ch, 2 A, 2 C, 4 A, 2 B, 4 A, 2 B, 4 A, 2 C, 2 A. Turn.

Kim Sayer

8th row 1ch, 1 A, 4 C, 2 A, 4 B, 2 A, 4 B, 2 A, 4 C, 1 A. Turn.
9th row As 8th.
10th row As 7th.
11th row 1ch, 5 A, 2 C, (4 A, 2 C) twice, 5 A. Turn.
12th row 1ch, 4 A, 4 C, 2 A, 4 B, 2 A, 4 C, 4 A. Turn.
13th row As 12th.
14th row As 11th.
15th-22nd rows As 7th-14th rows.
23rd and 24th rows Work in A. Fasten off.

To finish
Darn in ends. Join all plain motifs into a rectangle of 5 motifs by 6 motifs. Join colored motifs following chart at right for position. Fold batting into 3 equal layers, lay top section of cover on top of batting and pin all around. Cut batting slightly smaller than cover, then, using matching thread, machine stitch on RS of work across line of seams.
Place plain back of cover with RS out on batting, then with colored motifs uppermost using A and size E (3.50mm) hook, and working through both the front and back sections, work 1sc into each sc on short edges, 1sc into each row end on side edges, and 3sc into each corner, sl st into first sc. Turn.
Next round 1sc into each sc and 1sc into the center sc at each corner, sl st into first sc. Turn.
Rep last round twice more.
Picot round *1sc into each of next 3sc, 3ch, sl st into last sc made, rep from * all around, sl st into first sc.
Fasten off.
Press edging lightly.

1	2	3	4	1
1	4	2	3	1
1	3	4	2	1
1	2	3	4	1
1	4	2	3	1
1	3	4	2	1

* More Jacquard patterns
* Repeating a pattern
* Using separate balls of yarn
* Making a picture on a crochet fabric
* Stitch Wise: more Jacquard patterns
* Pattern for two vests

More Jacquard patterns

The Jacquard technique can be used in several different ways to create a variety of colorful designs on a crochet fabric. It is a good way to use up odds and ends of color, provided all the yarns are the same thickness, so that you achieve the same stitch gauge with each one. These colorful crochet fabrics could be used to make a number of household items or garments, including pillows, rugs and brightly patterned shawls. Try adding a bright Jacquard border to an otherwise plain sweater or cardigan. You could work a central design on a child's sweater or the pocket of a cardigan, or you might use a large bold pattern to work a vertical panel down the center of a bulky ski sweater.

The patterns should be worked in a plain, flat stitch like single crochet or half doubles to give clear definition to the shapes being worked, although a triple crochet fabric could be used if a very simple shape, like a square, is to be used to create the Jacquard effect.

Cross stitch embroidery patterns can be adapted quite successfully to crochet, since the outlines are usually clear and simple, and each X in the design can be used to represent a single stitch in the crochet fabric.

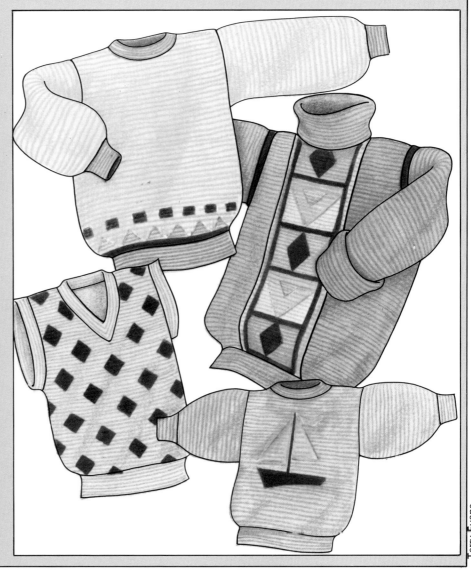

Terry Evans

Repeating a pattern

If you want to work a pattern all over the fabric, or repeat it several times—around the lower edge of a sweater, for example—it is much easier if the number of stitches needed to work the sweater is divisible by the number of stitches in one pattern repeat. For example, if the fabric is worked over 150 stitches, a pattern repeat consisting of 10 stitches in all would need to be repeated 15 times across the width of the fabric. If the pattern repeat cannot be divided easily in this way and there are stitches left over, it is important to center the design correctly before you start so that when you begin to work something like a neckline, in which the shaping cuts into the pattern, the pattern will be positioned symmetrically on each side of the center point.

Fred Mancini

Using separate balls of yarn

For a large pattern or picture in which several colors are used to make the design, you should use separate balls of yarn for each color. Cut a bobbin from heavy cardboard and wind the yarn onto it, taking the end of yarn through the notched end of the bobbin as shown here. By winding each color onto a separate bobbin, you will be able to keep the different colors from becoming tangled on the wrong side of the work.

You will find that it is worth spending a little extra time making the cardboard bobbins before you start working a Jacquard pattern, instead of simply winding small quantities of yarn from each large ball, since the bobbins make it much easier for you to control each color while it is being worked.

Fred Mancini

Making a picture on a crochet fabric

Choose a garment with as little shaping as possible so that you can concentrate on the design instead of worrying about complicated shaping while you work the various sections of the picture. You can use a ready-made graph like the one featured in this course to make one of the vests, or you can make your own pattern using a gauge sample and grid to help you. You will achieve the most accurate graph by drawing your own grid (see Volume 7, page 25). You could buy graph paper, but remember that the completed pattern will not be drawn to scale since the stitches are rectangular, not square. A graph paper design will appear elongated: the worked design will be wider and shorter than your pattern.

1 Make a gauge sample at least 7in (17.5cm) square in the stitch and yarn to be used for your design.

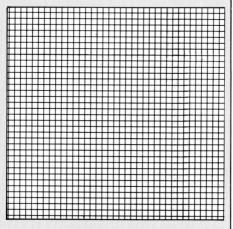

2 Draw a gauge grid on tracing paper so that the design can be easily transferred onto the grid using a fine pen (see Volume 7, page 25). Draw each box as accurately as possible to represent each stitch and row.

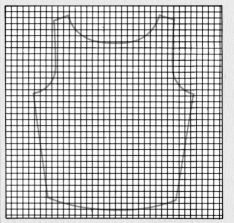

3 If your picture is to cover most of the crocheted fabric, chart out the shape of the garment on the grid so that you can see exactly how much space you will have available for your design.

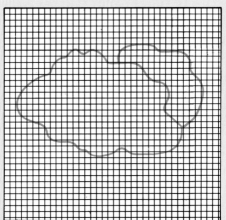

4 Draw or trace a rough outline of your picture on the gauge grid, using as few lines as possible. If you wish to include really small details, like the rays of the sun on our vest, for example, it would be better to embroider them on the fabric once it has been completed, using simple embroidery stitches and a large tapestry needle.

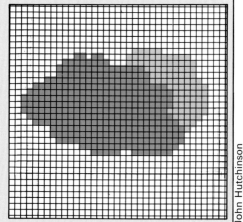

5 Now transfer the pattern onto the grid, coloring each section the same color as the yarn to be used to work the pattern as a reminder when you are working. Read the pattern from the chart in the normal way (see Volume 2, page 23). Start at the bottom right-hand corner and read RS rows from right to left and WS rows from left to right.

John Hutchinson

Stitch Wise

Overall patterns

These are two patterns which can be repeated to make a completely Jacquard fabric. Work in single crochet from the charts, starting at the bottom right-hand corner in the normal way and reading each RS row from right to left and each WS row from left to right. The pattern repeat has been marked on the chart in color, with the overall effect shown in black and white.

Motifs

These two simple motifs can be used as a center design on a sweater or can be incorporated into a fabric at any point. Use single crochet for these patterns to achieve the best results.

Borders

Here are two simple borders which can be worked around the bottom of a sweater or cardigan. Read the charts in the same way as when working the overall patterns. The pattern repeat has been shown on the chart in color, with the overall effect shown in black and white.

John Hutchinson

Fred Mancini

Sky high

You'll find these Jacquard vests fun to crochet and easy to wear —so why not make them both?

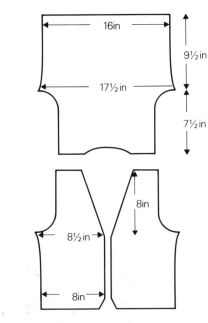

Brian Mayor

Sizes
To fit 32-34in (83-87cm) bust.
Length, 17in (42.5cm).

Materials
Sport yarn:
Cloud-scene vest *4 x 2oz (50g) balls
in main color (A)
1 ball each of 5 contrasting colors
(B, C, D, E and F)*
Geometric-patterned vest
*1 x 2oz (50g) ball in main color
(A)
2 balls in contrasting color (B)
1 ball in contrasting color (C)
1 ball in contrasting color (D)
No. 0 (2.00mm) steel hook
6 buttons*

Gauge
24 hdc and 18 rows to 4in (10cm) worked
on No. 0 (2.00mm) steel hook.

Note
These directions are for the basic shape
of both vests: follow the appropriate
chart on page 20 for the design you
want. It is easier to use small, separate
balls of yarn for individual sections
of color across a row than to strand
the yarn across the work.

Back
Using No. 0 (2.00mm) hook make 97ch.
Base row 1 hdc into 3rd ch from hook,
1 hdc into each ch to end. Turn. 96 sts.
Patt row 2ch to count as first hdc, 1 hdc

into each hdc, ending with last hdc into
2nd of 2ch. Turn.
Cont in patt, working from chart, until
26 rows have been completed. Inc one
st at each end of next and every foll 4th
row until there are 104 sts. Patt 3 more
rows.
Shape armholes
Next row Sl st into 9th hdc, 2ch, patt to
last 8 sts, turn.
Dec one st at each end of next 9 rows.
70 sts. Cont without shaping until 33
rows have been completed from beg of
armholes.
Shape back neck and shoulders
Next row 2ch, 1hdc into each of next
17hdc, turn.
Dec one st at neck edge on next 2 rows.
Fasten off.
Return to sts that were left, skip 34 sts
in center for back neck, rejoin yarn to
next st, 2ch, patt to end. Complete to
match first side.

Left front
Using No. 0 (2.00mm) hook make 45ch.
Work base row as for back. 44 sts.
Next row 2ch, 1hdc into st at base of ch,
1hdc into each hdc, ending with 1hdc
into 2nd of 2ch. Turn.
Next row Patt to last st, 2hdc into 2nd of
2ch. Turn.
Rep last 2 rows once more. 48 sts. Cont
in patt, working from chart, until 26 rows
have been completed. Inc one st at beg
of next and every foll 4th row until there
are 52 sts.
Shape front edge and armhole
Dec one st at beg (front edge) of next
and foll alternate row.
Next row Sl st into 9th hdc, 2ch, patt to
end. Turn.
Dec one st at armhole edge on next 9
rows, *at the same time* cont to dec at
front edge on next and every foll alternate
row until 16 sts rem. Cont without
shaping until 36 rows have been
completed from beg of armholes. Fasten
off.

Right front
Work as for left front, reversing all shaping.

To finish
Press or block according to yarn used.
Join shoulder and side seams.
Cloud-scene vest Work sc edging
around armholes and outer edge, using 1
round A and 2 rounds C: make 6 small
buttonholes on right front on last round.
Embroider sun's rays and raindrops in
stem stitch and birds in fly stitch.
Sew on buttons.
Geometric-patterned vest Work sc
edging around armholes using 1 round A
and 2 rounds C. Work sc edging around
outer edge, changing color with each
section, then 2 rounds C, making 6 small
buttonholes on right front on last round.
Sew on buttons.

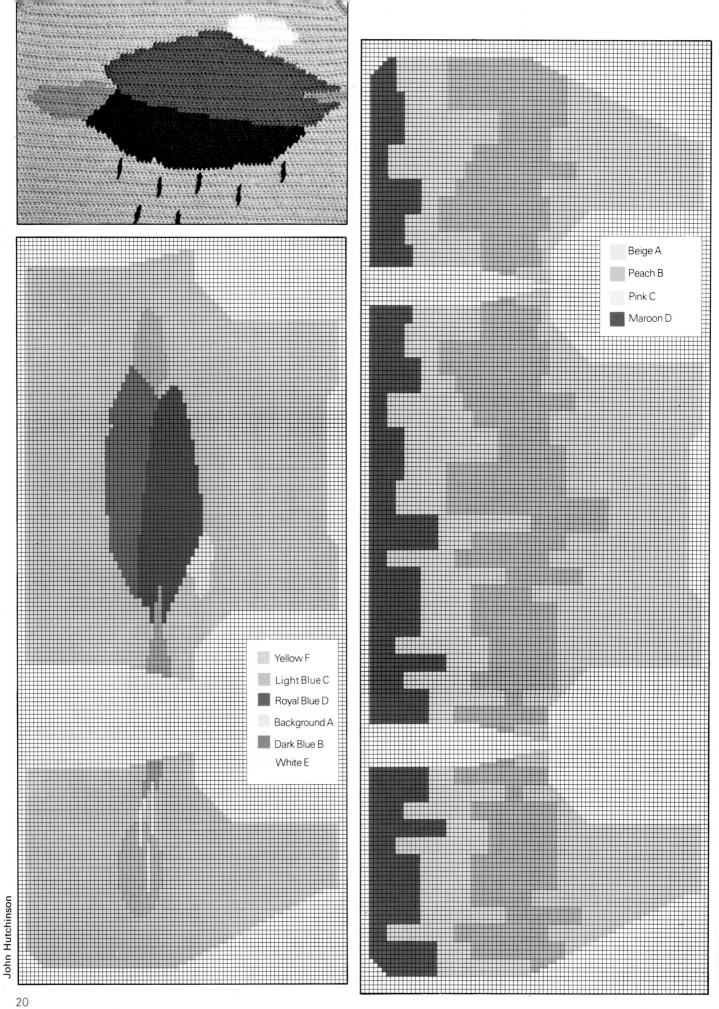

Yellow F
Light Blue C
Royal Blue D
Background A
Dark Blue B
White E

Beige A
Peach B
Pink C
Maroon D

John Hutchinson

Crochet / COURSE 41

Embossed motifs

You have already learned how to make circular and square motifs in a variety of patterns, using thick knitting yarns to create warm bulky fabrics or finer yarns and cottons for a lacy look. In this course we show you how to work bobbles, or popcorn stitches as they are sometimes called, on a plain square to achieve a highly textured finish. When they are sewn together, the squares make distinctive embossed fabrics, ideal for afghans, bedspreads and rugs.

You can work the squares in any firm yarn, from cotton for a beautifully textured lightweight fabric to knitting worsted yarn for a heavier fabric. You can use a bulky knitting yarn too, although the motifs create a very thick fabric when sewn together and are really only suitable for making something like a heavy rug.

You can vary the size of the motif by working fewer or more rounds where necessary. Remember to take into account the size of the motif and the yarn you would like to use when planning a design, since you would need to make a great many small squares for something like a bedspread, and in this case it might be better to increase the size of the motif by working more rounds.

To calculate the amount of yarn you will need for a particular design, work a sample square in the yarn and hook of your choice, making a note of how much yarn you have used for the square. Measure the size of your square, calculate how many you will need for your fabric and then work out the amount of yarn needed from these figures.

The basic square

The best results are achieved by working a very simple square, using doubles for the pattern so that the bobbles stand out clearly against the main fabric. We have used a sport yarn and a Size C (3.00mm) hook for our square, but you could use any odds and ends of yarn to make the sample.

1 Make 8 chains and join them into a circle with a slip stitch. Now make 3 chains and then work 27 doubles into the circle. 28 stitches including the first 3 chains. Join the last stitch to the 3rd of these chains with a slip stitch.

2 Begin the 2nd round with 3 chains. Skip the double at the base of these 3 chains. Now work a double into each of the next 6 doubles. 7 doubles in all. Now make 2 chains and then work a double into the next stitch for the first corner.

3 Continue working around the circle in this way, so that you work 3 more 2-chain corner loops with 7 doubles worked between each corner. Join the last chain to the top of the first 3 chains with a slip stitch. Join each round in the same way.

4 Start the next round in the same way as the last. Now work a double into each stitch made in the previous round, working 2 doubles, 2 chains and 2 doubles into each corner loop. You should now have 11 doubles on each side of the square.

5 Continue to work as many rounds as you like for the size of motif you need, so that you have 4 more doubles on each side of the square each time. Work the corners in the same way as the last round and work the end of each round in the correct pattern sequence. To finish the square, neatly work a round of doubles with 5 doubles worked into each corner loop.

Fred Mancini

Making the bobble

1 The bobble can be placed anywhere on the basic square, depending on the design of the motif. Work 5 doubles into the next stitch. Withdraw the hook from the loop and insert it from front to back under the two horizontal loops at the top of the first of these 5 doubles.

2 Insert the hook into the working loop again. Now wind the yarn over the hook and draw it through this loop and the first stitch, drawing the stitches firmly together to make a tight bobble—also called a popcorn.

3 On the following round work a double into the double horizontal loop at the *back* of the bobble, rather than into the front of it, so that it stands away from the main fabric.

Working embossed patterns

Now that you have learned how to work the plain square and the bobbles, you will have no difficulty in working the two squares featured in the cotton ponchos. You can, of course, create your own motif, and in this case it is a good idea to experiment with the yarn of your choice before beginning your design. For example, you may find it better to work a corner consisting of 1 double, 3 chains and 1 double when working with a fine yarn, or to work 2 doubles into the top of the bobble so that the motif remains flat.

1 To work a simple diamond pattern, work the first 2 rounds of the plain square. Now work a bobble into the 4th double (center) on each side of the motif on the next round. Be sure to include the double worked immediately after the bobble.

2 On the next round work a bobble into the stitch to the right of the center bobble. Now work a double into the back of the next bobble, followed by a bobble into the next stitch, so that you have worked 8 bobbles in this round.

3 Complete the diamond by working one more bobble on every round and a double in each bobble made in the previous rounds until it is the required size. To keep the pattern correct at the end of rounds count the number of doubles on each side, then complete the round accordingly, working a bobble as necessary.

4 Complete the square in the same way as the plain square, working the last round in doubles only, with 5 doubles worked into each corner loop.

5 Here a simple star motif has been worked, using the basic square and working a bobble at each side of the four corners, one stitch in from the 2-chain loop. Move each bobble one stitch toward the center on every round to achieve the four points of the star.

Joining the motifs

Fred Mancini

The motifs can be joined in several different ways depending on the effect you wish to achieve.
Here two motifs have been joined by overcasting the sides together with the same yarn that was used for the motifs, which creates an invisible seam.

These 2 motifs have been joined together with single crochet (see Volume 1, page 16) using a contrasting yarn to make a feature of the seam.

Here 2 motifs have been joined together using crab stitch (see Volume 4, page 25) and a contrasting yarn to create a raised seam. Hold the wrong side of the motifs together and work the crab stitch from left to right through both thicknesses.

Cotton ponchos for the poolside

Wear these crocheted ponchos right through the summer. They're great for lounging around the pool after a swim or over a sundress or pants.

Cluster motif poncho

Sizes
To fit 32-38in (81-96cm) bust.
Length, 31½in (80cm).

Materials
29oz (800g) of a medium-weight mercerized crochet cotton
Size B (2.50mm) crochet hook

Gauge
One motif measures approx 4½in (12cm) square worked on a size B (2.50mm) hook.

Cluster motif
Using size B (2.50mm) hook make 8 ch, join into a circle with a sl st.
1st round 3 ch, work 27dc into circle, join with a sl st to 3rd of first 3 ch.
2nd round 3ch to count as first dc, skip first dc, 1dc into each of next 6dc, *2ch, 1dc into each of next 7dc, rep from *, ending with 2ch. Join with a sl st to 3rd of first 3ch.
3rd round 3ch, skip first dc, 1dc into each of next 2dc, *5dc into next dc, remove

Victor Yuan

23

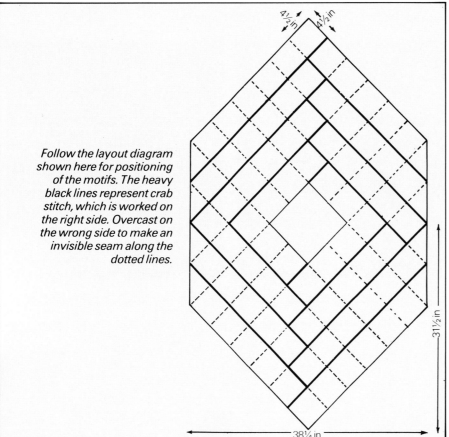

Follow the layout diagram shown here for positioning of the motifs. The heavy black lines represent crab stitch, which is worked on the right side. Overcast on the wrong side to make an invisible seam along the dotted lines.

John Hutchinson

4½ in   4½ in

31½ in

38¼ in

hook from loop and insert hook into first of the 5dc worked, replace dropped loop on hook, yo and draw a loop through—called 1 popcorn or 1pc—, 1dc into each of next 3dc, work 1dc, 3ch and 1dc all into next 2ch sp, 1dc into each of next 3dc, rep from * ending with 1 pc into next dc, 1dc into each of next 3dc, work 1dc, 3ch and 1dc all into last 2 ch sp, join with a sl st to 3rd of first 3 ch.

4th round 3ch, 1dc into next dc, *1pc into next dc, 2dc into next pc, 1pc into next dc, 1dc into each of next 3dc, work 1dc, 4ch and 1dc all into next 3ch sp—called 1dc group or 1grp—, 1dc into each of next 3dc, rep from * ending with 1grp into last 3ch sp, 1dc into next dc, join with a sl st to 3rd of first 3ch.

5th round 3ch, *1pc into next dc, 2dc into next pc, 1pc into next dc, 1dc into next dc, 1pc into next dc, 1pc into next dc, 1dc into each of next 3dc, 1grp into next 4ch sp, 1dc into each of next 3dc, rep from * ending with 1dc into each of last 2dc, join with a sl st to 3rd of first 3ch.

6th round Sl st into top of next pc, 3ch, 1dc into st at base of these 3ch, *(1pc into next dc, 1dc into next dc, 1dc into next pc) twice, 1pc into next dc, 1dc into each of next 3dc, 1grp into next 4ch sp, 1dc into each of next 3dc, 1pc into next dc, 2dc into next pc, rep from * to end, join with a sl st to 3rd of first 3ch.

7th round 3ch, 1pc into stitch at base of these 3ch, *(1dc into next dc, 1dc into next pc, 1dc into next pc) 3 times, 1dc

into each of next 3dc, 1grp into next 4ch sp, 1dc into each of next 3dc, 1pc into next dc, 2dc into next pc, 1pc into next dc, rep from *, ending with 2dc into last pc, join with a sl st to top of first pc.

8th round 3ch, work 1dc into each dc and 5dc into each 4ch sp all around, join with a sl st to 3rd of first 3ch.
Fasten off.
Make 75 more motifs in the same way.

Half motif

Note Half motifs are worked in rows instead of rounds so that there will be a right and wrong side to the fabric.
Using size B (2.50mm) hook make 6ch and join into a circle with a sl st.

1st row (RS) 3ch to count as first dc, work 15dc into circle, do not join. Turn.
2nd row 5ch to count as first dc and 2ch sp, skip first dc, 1dc into each of next 7dc, 2ch, 1dc into each of next 7dc, 2ch, 1dc into top of turning chain. Turn.
3rd row 6ch to count as first dc and 3ch sp, 1dc into first 2ch sp, *1dc into each of next 3dc, 1pc into next dc, 1dc into each of next 3dc, work 1dc, 3ch and 1dc all into next 2ch sp, rep from *, ending with 1dc, 3ch and 1dc into last sp. Turn.
4th row 6ch, 1dc into first 3ch sp, *1dc into each of next 3dc, work 5dc into next dc, drop loop from hook, insert hook into first of these 5dc from back of work (RS) to front of work (WS) and through

working loop, draw this loop through first dc—called 1 popcorn wrong side (1pcWS)—, (thus popcorn lies on RS of work), 2dc into next dc, 1pcWS into next dc, 1dc into each of next 3dc, work 1dc, 4ch and 1dc all into next 3ch sp—called 1 group (1grp)—, rep from *, ending with 1dc, 3ch and 1dc into last sp. Turn.
5th row 6ch, 1dc into first 3ch sp, *1dc into each of next 3dc, 1 pc into next dc, 2dc into next pc, 1 pc into next dc, 1dc into next dc and popcorn, 1pc into next dc, 1dc into each of next 3dc, 1grp into next 4ch sp, rep from * ending with 1dc, 3ch and 1dc into last sp. Turn.
6th row 6ch, 1dc into first sp, *1dc into each of next 3dc, 1pcWS into next dc, 2dc into next pc, (1pc into next dc, 1dc into each of next dc and pc) twice, 1pc into next dc, 1dc into each of next 3dc, 1grp into next 4ch sp, rep from *, ending with 1dc, 3ch and 1dc into last space. Turn.
7th row 5ch, 1dc into first 3ch sp, *1dc into each of next 3dc, 1 pc into next dc, 2dc into next pc, (1 pc into next dc, 1dc into each of next dc and pc) 3 times, 1 pc into next dc, 1dc into each of next 3dc, 1grp into next 4ch sp, rep from *, ending with 1dc, 3ch and 1dc into last sp. Turn.
8th row 3ch, 3dc into first 3ch sp, work 1dc into each dc and 5dc into each 4ch corner sp all around, ending with 4dc into last 3ch sp. Fasten off.
Make 7 more half motifs in the same way.

Poncho

Darn all loose ends into wrong side of motifs.
Join the motifs as shown in the diagram. Use a blunt-ended yarn needle and the same yarn to overcast the motifs joined with a dotted line on the chart. Use crab stitch (see Volume 4, page 25) and the same yarn to join the motifs on the right side of the work (indicated on the diagram with a solid line) to create a raised diagonal seam.

Neckband

With RS of work facing, rejoin yarn to left shoulder at neck edge and work 10 rows sc all around neck edge, dec 1sc at each corner on every row to shape edging.

Lower border

With right side of work facing, rejoin yarn to left-hand side of poncho at armhole edge and work 15 rows sc around lower edge, inc 2sc at lower point on every row by working 2sc into one stitch at point, and dec 1sc at lower armhole points on every row.
Work around other side in same way.
With WS of work facing, overcast lower edge of each armhole together for 31½in (80cm).

Victor Yuan

Star motif poncho

Sizes
To fit 32-38in (81-96cm) bust.
Length, 31½in (80cm)

Materials
*29oz (800g) of a medium-weight
   mercerized crochet cotton
Size B (2.50mm) crochet hook*

Gauge
One motif measures approx 4½in (12cm)
square worked on a size B (2.50mm) hook.

Star motif

Using size B (2.50mm) hook make 8
chains, join into a circle with a sl st.
1st round 3ch to count as first dc, work
27dc into circle, join with a sl st to 3rd of
first 3 ch.
2nd round 3ch, skip first dc, 1dc into each
of next 6dc, *2ch, 1dc into each of next
7dc, rep from *, ending with 2ch, join
with a sl st to 3rd of first 3ch.
3rd round 3ch, skip first dc, 1dc into each
of next 6dc, work 2dc, 2ch and 2dc all into
next 2ch sp at corner—called 1 group or
1grp—, *1dc into each of next 7dc, 1grp
into next 2ch sp, rep from * to end, join
with a sl st to 3rd of first 3ch.
4th round 3ch, 1dc into each of next 6dc,
*5dc into next dc, drop loop from hook,
insert hook into first of these 5dc and
back into dropped loop, yo and draw
through a loop—called 1 popcorn or
1pc—(see page 22), 1dc into next dc.
1grp into next 2ch sp, 1dc into next dc,
1pc into next dc, 1dc into each of next
7dc, rep from *, ending with 1 pc into last
dc, join with a sl st to 3rd of first 3ch.
5th round Sl st into next dc, 3ch, 1dc into
each of next 4dc, *1pc into next dc, 1dc
into tip of next pc, 1dc into each of next
3dc, 1grp into next 2ch sp, 1dc into each
of next 3dc, 1dc into tip of next pc, 1pc
into next dc, 1dc into each of next 5dc,
rep from * ending with 1pc into last dc,
join with a sl st to 3rd of first 3ch.
6th round Sl st into next dc, 3ch, 1dc into
each of next 2dc, *1pc into next dc, 1dc
into tip of next pc, 1dc into each of next
6dc, 1grp into next 2ch sp, 1dc into each
of next 6dc, 1dc into tip of next pc, 1 pc
into next dc, 1dc into each of next 3dc,
rep from *, ending with 1 pc into last dc,
join with a sl st to 3rd of first 3ch.
7th round 3ch, 1pc into same place as
sl st, 1dc into next dc, *1pc into next dc,
1dc into tip of next pc, 1dc into each of
next 9dc, 3dc into next 2ch sp, 1dc into
each of next 9dc, 1dc into next pc, 1 pc
into next dc, 1dc into next dc, rep from *
working last dc into tip of last pc, join
with a sl st to top of first pc.
8th round Sl st into next dc, 3ch, 1 pc into
stitch at base of these 3ch, *1dc into tip
of next pc, 1dc into each of next 11dc,
3dc into next dc, 1dc into each of next

11dc, 1dc into tip of next pc, 1pc into next dc, rep from * to end, join with a sl st to top of first pc. Fasten off. Make 75 more motifs in same way.

Half motif

Note Half motifs are worked in rows rather than rounds so that there will be a right and wrong side to the fabric.
Using size B (2.50mm) hook make 6 chains, join into a circle with a sl st.
1st row (RS) 3ch, work 15 dc into ring, do not join. Turn.
2nd row 5ch to count as first dc and 2ch sp, skip first dc, *1dc into each of next 7 dc, 2ch, rep from * once more, 1dc into top of turning chain. Turn.
3rd row 5ch, 2dc into first 2ch sp, *1dc into each of next 7dc, work 2dc, 2ch and 2dc all into next 2ch sp—called 1 group or 1grp—, rep from * ending with 2dc into last 2ch sp, 2ch, 1dc into 3rd of first 5ch. Turn.
4th row 5ch, 2dc into first 2ch sp, *1dc into next 5dc, 5dc into next dc, drop loop from hook, insert hook into first of these 5dc from back of work (RS) to front of work (WS) and through working loop, draw this loop through first dc—called 1 popcorn wrong side (1 pcWS)—, 1dc into each of next 7dc, 1 pcWS into next dc, 1dc into next dc, 1grp into next 2ch sp, rep from *, ending with 2dc into last 2ch sp, 1dc into 3rd of first 5ch. Turn.
5th row 5ch, 2dc into first 2ch sp, *1dc into each of next 3dc, 1dc into next pc, 1 pc (on RS of work, see star motif), into next dc, 1dc into each of next 5dc, 1pc into next dc, 1dc into tip of next pc, 1dc into each of next 3dc, 1grp into next 2ch sp, rep from * ending with 2dc into last 2ch sp, 2ch, 1dc into 3rd of first 5ch. Turn.
6th row 5ch, 2dc into first 2ch sp, *1dc into each of next 6dc, 1dc into next pc, 1 pcWS into next dc, 1dc into each of next 3dc, 1 pcWS into next dc, 1dc into next pc, 1dc into each of next 6dc, 1grp into next 2ch sp, rep from * ending with 2dc into last 2ch sp, 2ch, 1dc into 3rd of first 5ch. Turn.
7th row 3ch, 2dc into first 2ch sp, *1dc into each of next 9dc, 1dc into next pc, 1 pc into next dc, 1dc into next dc, 1 pc into next dc, 1dc into tip of next pc, 1dc into each of next 9dc, 3dc into next 2ch sp, rep from * ending with 2dc into last 2ch sp, 1dc into 3rd of first 5ch. Turn.
8th row 3ch, 2dc into next dc, *1dc into each of next 11dc, 1dc into tip of next pc, 1pc into next dc, 1dc into tip of next pc, 1dc into each of next 11dc, 3dc into next dc, rep from *, ending with 2dc into last dc, 1dc into 3rd of first 3ch.
Fasten off.
Work 7 more half motifs in same way.

Poncho
Complete as for cluster motif poncho.

Victor Yuan

Shoestring

Button bonanza

Give children's clothes an individual look with a set of embroidered buttons. Choose flowers or faces.

Materials

- *Self-cover button kits in different sizes*
- *Scraps of matching or contrasting fabric*
- *White backing fabric*
- *Stranded embroidery floss in a variety of colors*
- *Tracing paper*
- *Dressmaker's carbon paper*

1 Place the chosen fabric over the white backing fabric with wrong sides together. Pin and baste together to hold.

2 Lightly pencil circles of the correct size and number on the fabric, following the kit instructions for the size of the circles.

3 Using pencil, lightly draw a design in the center of each circle, making sure that the design will be on the front of the button when it is completed.

4 To use the designs shown here, trace the design and, using dressmaker's carbon, mark the design in the center of the fabric circle.

5 Use three strands of embroidery floss throughout. Work each design using a variety of stitches.

6 Work the faces on the children's buttons in chain stitch, back stitch, satin stitch and French knots, in the colors shown.

7 The flower buttons are worked in lazy daisy stitch, straight stitch and French knots, in the colors shown.

8 Cut out each circle. Trim away the white backing fabric, leaving it the size of the button face.

9 Assemble the buttons following the instructions supplied with the kit and sew them to the garment.

Brian Nash

28

Making a diagonal pocket opening

Diagonal lines, which might be called for on a pocket opening on a jacket or cardigan, may be formed across a knitted fabric by turning the work before a row of knitting is completed. Sometimes this method is known as "short-row knitting". You can achieve any angle by turning the work; if you increase the number of unworked stitches by one on alternate rows, then the diagonal line will be very steep. Leaving a larger group of stitches unworked each time diminishes the angle.

Make a diagonal line sloping upward to the right by turning the knitting on a right-side row; a line sloping upward to the left must be turned on the wrong side of the fabric. The Guernsey-style jackets on page 32 have directions for a diagonal type of pocket opening: the step-by-step photographs here are based on those directions.

1 First make a pocket lining according to the pattern. Work the left front straight in stockinette stitch as instructed in the pattern, ending with a knit row. On the following row, purl to the last few stitches (in this case, two stitches). Leave these stitches unworked and turn the work as though you were at the end of a row.

2 Knit to the end of the next row. Continue to repeat the last two rows, working a few stitches less each time on every purl row and then turning the work. Here the third turn is complete: note that unworked stitches on the right-hand needle are already slanting.

3 This is how the fabric looks just before you insert the pocket lining when the shaping is almost complete. Gradually increasing the number of unworked stitches (to 10 here) at one edge makes a distinctive wedge-shaped fabric.

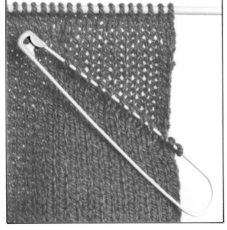

4 Insert the pocket lining on the next row: purl to the last 12 stitches, slip these stitches onto a holder for the pocket top, then purl across the 12 stitches of the pocket lining. Continue in stockinette stitch across all the stitches.

5 When the garment is complete, work a ribbed pocket top as directed in the instructions. Any slight holes in the fabric—resulting from turning the work in the middle of a row—are disguised when the ribbing draws the stitches together.

Fred Mancini

Introduction to Guernsey and fishermen's knitting

In centuries past, the ports around Britain produced fishermen's garments, usually rough working sweaters, often made by the men themselves. The original garments came from the sister islands of Guernsey and Jersey.

The sweaters were always a similar shape with dropped shoulders and square arm-holes; they were knitted in rounds with underarm and often neck gussets for extra movement. Thick, oiled wool in the traditional navy-blue color was used on fine needles to make a hard-wearing fabric that was warm and kept out the wet and the cold. The sweaters were ideally suited to the rough weather endured by the fishermen.

Today Guernsey sweaters are popular for casual wear. There is no need for such a tough fabric, but a similar effect can be achieved with good quality knitting worsted yarn and needles two sizes smaller than you would normally use for that type of yarn. The main fabric is always stockinette stitch decorated with stitch patterns, to which the fine needles and thick yarn lend a brocade effect. Stitch patterns are often enclosed in horizontal or vertical bands of knitting separated by cables on a simple textured

background fabric. The main patterned sections are usually the front and back yokes of the sweater. The sleeve tops may also be patterned. The patterns are usually simple knit and purl textures and vary from region to region. But all the designs—flags, ladders, cables, trees and plants—trace their origins to nature and seafaring life.

Background photograph: Frank Sutcliffe Gallery

Tree of life

Based on pinecone or fern, this classic stitch pattern originated in the Scottish Fair Isles and is typical of the natural images found in fishermen's knitting.

The pattern is set in a panel 15 sts wide.
1st row (RS) K7, P1, K7.
2nd row P6, K1, P1, K1, P6.
3rd row K5, P1, K3, P1, K5.
4th row P4, (K1, P2) twice, K1, P4.
5th row K3, P1, K2, P1, K1, P1, K2, P1, K3.
6th row (P2, K1) twice, P3, (K1, P2) twice.
7th row K1, P1, (K2, P1) 4 times, K1.
8th row P3, K1, P2, K1, P1, K1, P2, K1, P3.
9th row (K2, P1) twice, K3, (P1, K2) twice.
10th row As 4th.
11th row As 5th.
12th row P5, K1, P3, K1, P5.
13th row K4, (P1, K2) twice, P1, K4.
14th row As 2nd.
15th row As 3rd.
16th row P7, K1, P7.
17th row K6, P1, K1, P1, K6.
18th row P to end.
19th row As first.
20th row P to end.
These 20 rows form the patt. Rep them throughout.

Betty Martin

Double ribbing and stockinette stitches combine to give a honeycomb effect suitable for using in a panel between other stitches or as a fabric in its own right.
Cast on a multiple of 4 sts plus 2 extra.
1st row (RS) K2, *P2, K2, rep from * to end.
2nd row P2, *K2, P2, rep from * to end.
3rd row K to end.
4th row P to end.
These 4 rows form the patt. Rep them throughout.

Wise

Double seed stitch

Flag pattern

This allover pattern is a combination of seed stitch and double ribbing: it is used as a background between panels of other stitches.

Cast on a multiple of 4 sts plus 2 extra.

1st row K2, *P2, K2, rep from * to end.
2nd row P2, *K2, P2, rep from * to end.
3rd row As 2nd.
4th row As first.

These 4 rows form the patt. Rep them throughout.

The triangular shape of the flag may vary in width and depth: on the right it is worked in reverse stockinette stitch on a stockinette stitch background and on the left is knitted against a purl background. These directions are for the flag on the right which is set in a panel of 8 sts. Simply read P for K and vice versa if you want the flag on the left.

1st row (RS) K1, P7.
2nd row K6, P2.
3rd row K3, P5.

4th row P4, K4.
5th row K5, P3.
6th row K2, P6.
7th row K7, P1.
8th row P to end.

These 8 rows form the patt. Rep them throughout.

Fred Mancini

31

Great Guernseys

Take your choice of pattern panels to make a handsome, hard-wearing Guernsey-style jacket.

Sizes

To fit 24 [26:28:30]in (61[66:71:76]cm) chest.
Length, 16 [17½:19:20½]in (40 [44:48:52]cm).
Sleeve seam, 12½ [13½:14½:15¾]in (31 [34:37:40]cm).
Note Directions for larger sizes are in brackets []; where there is only one set of figures it applies to all sizes.

Materials

10[11:12:13] x 2oz (50g) balls of a knitting worsted
1 pair each Nos. 7 and 9 (5 and 6mm) knitting needles; Cable needle
14[16:16:19]in (35[40:40:48]cm) open-ended zipper

Gauge

16 sts and 20 rows to 4in (10cm) in stockinette st on No. 9 (6mm) needles.
Note All patt panels are referred to in the directions as "patt 11[11:13:13]". Choose two panels—one for each side of center front opening and hood and the other to form the front and back yokes. Here 4 stitches are worked between each.

Patt panel A

1st row P1, (K1, P1) 5[5:6:6] times.
2nd row K2, (P1, K1) 4[4:5:5] times. K1.
Rep these 2 rows throughout.

Patt panel B

1st row P1, K9[9:11:11], P1.
2nd row K1, P9[9:11:11], K1.
3rd row P to end.
4th row K to end.
Rep these 4 rows throughout.

Patt panel C

1st row P1[1:2:2], K4, P1, K4, P1 [1:2:2].
2nd row K1[1:2:2], P3, K1, P1, K1, P3, K1[1:2:2].
3rd row P1[1:2:2], K2, (P1, K1) twice, P1, K2, P1[1:2:2].
4th row K1[1:2:2], P1, (K1, P1) 4 times, K1[1:2:2].
5th row As 3rd.
6th row As 2nd.
7th row As first.
8th row K1[1:2:2], P9, K1[1:2:2].
Rep these 8 rows throughout.

Patt panel D

Fred Mancini

1st row P1 [1:2:2], K1, P1, K7, P1 [1:2:2].
2nd row K1 [1:2:2], P6, K1, P2, K1 [1:2:2].
3rd row P1 [1:2:2], K3, P1, K5, P1 [1:2:2].
4th row K1 [1:2:2], P4, K1, P4, K1 [1:2:2].
5th row P1 [1:2:2], K5, P1, K3, P1 [1:2:2].
6th row K1 [1:2:2], P2, K1, P6, K1 [1:2:2].
7th row P1 [1:2:2], K7, P1, K1, P1 [1:2:2].
8th row As 6th.
9th row As 5th.
10th row As 4th.
11th row As 3rd.
12th row As 2nd.
Rep these 12 rows throughout.

Back
Using No. 7 (5mm) needles cast on 53[57:61:65] sts.
1st row K1, *P1, K1, rep from * to end.
2nd row P1, *K1, P1, rep from * to end.
Rep these 2 rows 3 times more. Change to No. 9 (6mm) needles. Beg with a K row, cont in stockinette st until work measures 9½[10½:12:13]in (24[27:30: 33]cm); end with K row. Change to No. 7 (5mm) needles. K4 rows.
Next row K2[4:2:4], *K into front and back of next st—called inc 1, K1, inc 1, K7[7:9:9], inc 1, K1, rep from * 3 times more, inc 1, K2[4:2:4]. 66[70:74:78] sts. Change to No. 9 (6mm) needles. Beg yoke patt.
1st row P1[3:1:3], *K4, patt 11[11:13:13], rep from * 3 times more, K4, P1[3:1:3].
2nd row K1[3:1:3], *P4, patt 11[11:13:13], rep from * 3 times more, P4, K1[3:1:3].
3rd row P1[3:1:3], * sl next 2 sts onto cable needle and leave at back of work, K2, then K2 from cable needle—called C4, patt 11[11:13:13], rep from * 3 times more, C4, P1[3:1:3].

Victor Yuan

4th row As 2nd.
Keeping patt panels correct, rep last 4 rows until work measures 16[17½:19: 20½]in (40[44:48:52]cm); end with WS row.

Shape shoulders
Bind off 8[8:9:9] sts at beg of next 4 rows and 7[8:7:8] sts at beg of foll 2 rows. Bind off rem 20[22:24:26] sts.

Left front
Using No. 9 (6mm) needles cast on 12[14:14:16] sts for pocket lining. Beg with a K row, work 4¾[5:5:5½]in (12[13: 13:14]cm) stockinette st; end with K row. Cut off yarn and leave sts on a holder. Using No. 7 (5mm) needles cast on 27[29:31:33] sts.
1st row *K1, P1, rep from * to last 3 sts, K3.
2nd row K2, P1, *K1, P1, rep from * to end.
Rep these 2 rows twice more, then the first of them again.
Next row K2, P into front and back of next st—called inc 1 P-wise, rib 7[7:9:9], inc 1 P-wise, K1, inc 1 P-wise, rib to end. 30[32:34:36] sts.
Change to No. 9 (6mm) needles. Beg patt panel.
1st row K12[14:14:16], P1, K4, patt 11[11:13:13], K2.
2nd row K2, patt 11[11:13:13], P4, K1, P to end.
3rd row K12[14:14:16], P1, C4, patt 11[11:13:13], K2.
4th row As 2nd.
Rep these 4 rows until work measures 2¾[3:3:3½]in (7[8:8:9]cm) from end of ribbing; end with RS row.

Shape pocket opening
Next row Work to last 2 sts, turn.
Next row Work to end.
Next row Work to last 4 sts, turn.
Cont to work 2 sts less on every other row 3[4:4:5] times more; end with RS row.
Next row Patt to last 12[14:14:16] sts, leave rem sts on a holder and P across sts of pocket lining.
Cont across all sts until work measures 9½[10½:12:13]in (24[27:30:33]cm) from beg; end with a 3rd row (i.e. cable row).
Next row Patt 17[17:19:19], change to No. 7 (5mm) needle and K to end.
Next row K13[15:15:17], change to No. 9 (6mm) needle and patt to end.
Rep last 2 rows once more.
Next row Patt 17[17:19:19], change to No. 7 (5mm) needle, inc 1, K7[7:9:9], inc 1, K1, inc 1, K2[4:2:4]. 33[35:37:39] sts.
Change to No. 9 (6mm) needles.
Next row P1[3:1:3], *K4, patt 11[11:13:13], rep from * once more, K2.
Cont in patt as set until work measures 14[15½:16½:18]in (35[39:42:46]cm) from beg; end with RS row.

Shape neck
Bind off 5[6:6:7] sts at beg of next row and 2 sts at beg of foll alternate row. Dec one st at end of next and foll 2[2:3:3] alternate rows. Work 1[1:3:3] rows, ending at armhole edge.

Shape shoulder
Bind off 8[8:9:9] sts at beg of next and foll alternate row. Work 1 row. Bind off rem 7[8:7:8] sts.

Right front
Work pocket lining for left front, but ending with a P row. Using No. 7 (5mm) needles cast on 27[29:31:33] sts.
1st row K3, *P1, K1, rep from * to end.
2nd row *P1, K1, rep from * to last 3 sts, P1, K2.
Rep these 2 rows twice more, then the first of them again.
Next row Rib 14[16:16:18], inc 1 P-wise, rib 7[7:9:9], inc 1 P-wise, K2. 30[32:34:36] sts.
Change to No. 9 (6mm) needles.
Next row K2, patt 11[11:13:13], K4, P1, K to end.
Cont to match left, reversing shaping.

Sleeves
Using No. 7 (5mm) needles cast on 29[31:33:35] sts. Work 8 rows ribbing as for back. Change to No. 9 (6mm) needles. Beg with a K row, cont in stockinette st, inc one st at each end of 3rd and every foll 5th row until there are 45[49:53:57] sts. Cont without shaping until sleeve seam measures 12[13:14:15¼]in (30[33:36:39]cm) from beg; end with K row. K3 rows. Bind off loosely.

Hood
Using No. 9 (6mm) needles cast on 69[73:79:83] sts.
1st row K2, patt 11[11:13:13], K4, P1, K to last 18[18:20:20] sts, P1, K4, patt 11[11:13:13], K2.
2nd row K2, patt 11[11:13:13], P4, K1, P to last 18[18:20:20] sts, K1, P4, patt 11[11:13:13], K2.
3rd row K2, patt 11[11:13:13], C4, P1, K to last 18[18:20:20] sts, P1, C4, patt 11[11:13:13], K2.
4th row As 2nd.
Rep these 4 rows until work measures 7[7½:8:8½]in (18[19:21:22]cm); end with WS row.

Shape top
Next row Patt 32[34:37:39], sl 1, K1, psso, K1, K2 tog, patt to end.
Next row Patt to end.
Cont to dec in center of next and every other row 3[3:4:4] times more; end with RS row. 61[65:69:73] sts.
Next row Patt 28[30:32:34], P2 tog, P1, P2 tog tbl, patt to end. Cont to dec at center of row 3[4:4:5] times more. Bind off.

Pocket borders
Using No. 7 (5mm) needles and with RS of work facing, K across 12[14:14:16] sts on holder, inc one st at each end and at center of row. 15[17:17:19] sts. Beg with a first row, 4 rows rib as for back. Bind off in ribbing. Finish off pockets.

To finish
Press or block according to yarn used. Join shoulder seams. Sew in sleeves and zipper. Join hood seam and sew hood to neck. Press seams.

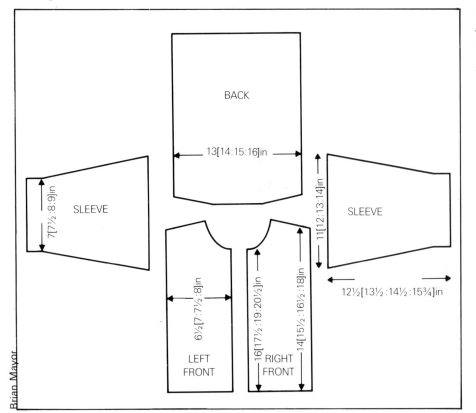

BACK

13[14:15:16]in

SLEEVE

SLEEVE

7½[7½:8:9]in

11[12:13:14]in

12½[13½:14½:15¾]in

LEFT FRONT

RIGHT FRONT

6½[7:7½:8]in

16[17½:19:20½]in

14[15½:16½:18]in

Brian Mayor

Knitting/COURSE 40

*Formation of a fisherman's sweater
*Working an underarm gusset
*Pattern for His and Hers Guernseys

Formation of a fisherman's sweater

There are a number of different ways of constructing a Guernsey-style sweater, but the principle is the same for all of them—for added strength, the body is knitted in rounds on a circular needle, while the sleeves are worked downward in rounds on a set of four needles using stitches picked up around the armholes. There are enough stitches in the body to use a circular needle effectively, but the smaller number of sleeve stitches must be worked on a set of needles.

In the Guernsey-style sweaters on page 37 the work is divided at the armholes, then the back and front are completed separately in rows. Other designs may be worked entirely in rounds with the armhole division marked only by long horizontal strands of yarn made by winding the yarn several times around the needle on one round and dropping the extra loops on the next rounds. When the body is complete, the strands are cut down the center to open the armhole. Each strand is darned in on the wrong side of the work before the sleeve stitches are picked up around the armhole.

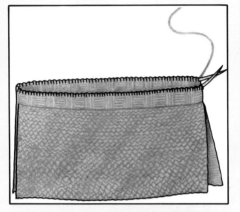

1 The lower edge of the body often consists of two separate flaps which give extra movement. The flaps are knitted on a pair of needles in garter stitch to make a firm lower edge on the garment. Begin the tubular fabric of the body by joining the flaps on a circular needle and proceed in rounds. Here there is a narrow ribbed trimming immediately above the garter stitch.

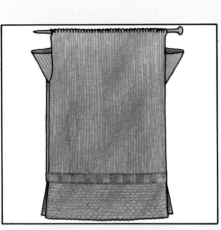

2 The body is worked in rounds on a circular needle: a vertical row of single purl stitches on each side above the slits marks the side "seams." Still working in rounds, shape the underarm gussets (see page 36). After the gussets are complete, the work is divided so that you finish the back and front separately: leave the gusset stitches on a length of thread then use a pair of needles to knit the back and front in rows.

Terry Evans

3 Complete the back and front sections in the same way: knit straight, without any shaping, to the shoulders. Bind off stitches at each end of the needle for the shoulders, then continue in ribbing on the center stitches for a small stand-up neckband. Usually Guernsey-style stitch patterns are worked across the front and back sections of the garment from the underarm upward.

4 The sleeves are also knitted in rounds working in a downward direction from the armholes. Join the shoulder seams. Using a set of needles, pick up the sleeve stitches from around the armholes, including the gusset stitches. As the sleeve progresses downward the gusset stitches are gradually decreased.

5 One stitch remaining from the gusset forms the "seam" stitch of the sleeve. Just as an ordinary sleeve is shaped, so the Guernsey sleeve is narrowed toward the cuff by decreasing on each side of the seam stitch at regular intervals. The last part of the sleeve before binding off consists of a ribbed cuff.

Fred Mancini

Working an underarm gusset

An underarm gusset is a diamond-shaped piece of knitting set into the side seam of a garment before the armhole division and eventually carried on into the top of the sleeve. The kind of gusset shown here is a feature of Guernsey-style sweaters where the body and sleeves are knitted in rounds: they are worked as part of the main fabric and not as a separate inset.

Most of the original fishermen's garments were made of thick yarn and were close-fitting for extra warmth: a gusset allowed for movement and for ease in dressing and undressing.

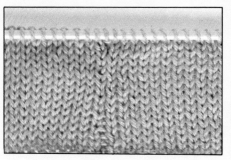

1 When you knit the body of a Guernsey in rounds of stockinette stitch (here it is shown flat for clarity), the side seams are marked by a vertical line of single purl stitches; these leave only a slight definition as the purl stitches sink into the fabric.

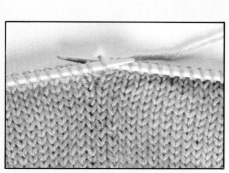

2 To start shaping the gusset, knit to the position of the seam stitch. Increase one stitch on each side of the seam stitch by first picking up the strand lying between the two needles and knitting it through the back of the loop; knit the original seam stitch, then increase another stitch in the same way as before.

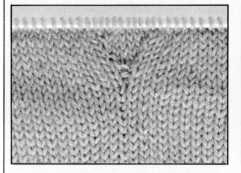

3 At the end of the first shaping round, the gusset grows from the center of the side seam and consists of 3 stitches. On the following alternate rounds, increase one stitch on each side of the gusset stitches in the same way as before—this way the gusset gains two new stitches on alternate rounds. Here there are 9 stitches in the gusset.

4 When the gusset is complete—here it has 17 stitches—work across the stitches once more after the last increase, then slip them on a stitch holder. You can no longer knit in rounds: complete the back and front sections separately on a pair of needles as instructed in the pattern.

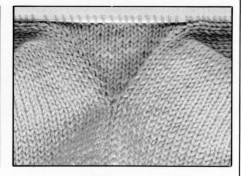

5 After you finish the body of the sweater, join the shoulder seams. Refer to the pattern directions and, using a set of 4 needles, knit across the gusset stitches, then pick up stitches all around the armhole. Here the work is shown flat so that you can see it more clearly.

6 You are now working a sleeve downward in rounds from the armholes. The gusset in the body underarm extends into the sleeve: these gusset stitches must be gradually decreased. Work across the gusset stitches in this way— sl1, K1, psso, K to last 2 gusset sts, K2 tog—so decreasing one stitch at each end of the gusset.

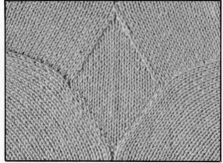

7 Continue to decrease in this way on alternate rounds until one gusset stitch is left. This remaining stitch becomes the seam stitch of the sleeve—you must purl it on subsequent rounds. The gusset is now complete and should be a neat diamond shape when it is flat.

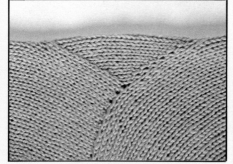

8 When the gusset is complete, the fabric folds neatly at the body and sleeve seam stitches. The gusset also folds in half to form a triangular inset bridge between body and sleeve at the underarm.

Fred Mancini

Rain or shine

These versatile unisex Guernsey sweaters are a stylish and comfortable way to keep warm on a chilly day.

Sizes

To fit 32[34:36:38:40:42]in (83[87:92:97:102:107]cm) bust/chest.
Length, 24[25:26:26½:27:28]in (61[63:65:67:69:71]cm).
Underarm sleeve measures 18[18½:19:19½:20:20½]in (46[47:48:49:50:51]cm).
Note Directions for larger sizes are in brackets []; if there is only one set of figures, it applies to all sizes.

Materials

22[23:25:26:28:29] x 1oz (25g) balls of a knitting worsted
1 pair each Nos. 3 and 4 (3¼ and 3¾mm) knitting needles
Nos. 3 and 4 (3¼ and 3¾mm) circular needles
Set of four Nos. 3 and 4 (3¼ and 3¾mm) double-pointed needles
Cable needle; stitch holder

Tony Boase

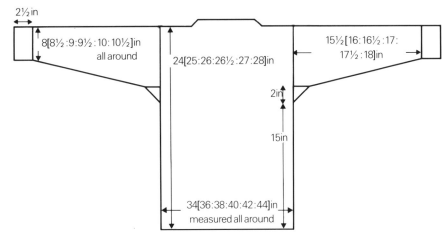

Brian Mayor

Gauge
24 sts and 32 rows to 4in (10cm) in stockinette st on No. 4 (3¾mm) needles.

Back and front
Using No. 3 (3¼mm) needles cast on 103 [109:115:121:127:133] sts. Work 4in (10cm) garter st; end with WS row. Cut off yarn and leave sts for time being. Work a second piece in same way, but do not cut off yarn. Using No. 3 (3¼mm) circular needle K across 2nd piece to last st, K last st tog with first st of other piece, then K to last st of other piece, K last st tog with first st of first piece. 204[216:228:240:252:264] sts.

Next round *K2, P2, rep from * to end. Rep last round once more. K2 rounds. Rep these 4 rounds once more, then work first 2 rounds again. Change to No. 4 (3¾mm) circular needle.

Next round Pick up loop lying between needles and K tbl—called make one or M1, K102[108:114:120:126:132], M1, K102[108:114:120:126:132]. 2 sts increased.

Next round K to end.

Next round *P1, K102[108:114:120: 126:132], rep from * once more. Rep last 2 rounds until work measures 15in (38cm) from beg.

Shape gusset
Next round *M1, K1, M1, K102[108: 114:120:126:132], rep from * once more.

Next round K to end.

Next round *M1, K3, M1, K102[108: 114:120:126:132], rep from * once more. Cont to inc in this way at each side of both gussets on every other round until there are 238[250:262:274:286: 298] sts; end with inc round.

Next round K17 and sl these sts onto a holder, K102[108:114:120:126:132], turn and cont on these sts for back. Change to No. 3 (3¼mm) needles. K 3 rows, dec one st in center of last row on 2nd size, inc one st in center on 3rd and 6th sizes and inc one st at each end on 5th size. 102[107:115:120:128:133] sts. Change to No. 4 (3¾mm) needles. Beg yoke patt.

1st row *P2, K6[6:10:10:14:14], P2, K1, M1, K2, M1, K1, P2, K10, P2, K5, P1, K5, P2 **, (P2, K3) 4[5:5:6:6:7] times, rep from ** back to *. 106[111: 119:124:132:137] sts.

2nd row *K2, P6[6:10:10:14:14], K2, P6, K2, P10, K2, P5, K1, P5, K2 **, K1, (P3, K2) 3[4:4:5:5:6] times, P3, K1, rep from ** back to *.

3rd row *(P2, K2) 2[2:3:3:4:4] times, P2, sl next 3 sts onto cable needle and leave at back of work, K3, then K the sts from cable needle—called cable 6 back or C6B, P2, (K2, P2) 3 times, K4, P1, K1, P1, K4, P2 **, (K3, P2) 4[5:5:6:6:7] times, rep from ** back to * but work C6F (sl next 3 sts onto cable needle and leave at front of work, K3, then K the sts from cable needle) instead of C6B.

4th row *(K2, P2) 2[2:3:3:4:4] times, K2, P6, K2, (P2, K2) 3 times, P4, K1, P1, K1, P4, K2 **, P1, (K2, P3) 3[4:4:5:5: 6] times, K2, P2, rep from ** back to *.

5th row * P2, K6[6:10:10:14:14], P2, K6, P2, K10, P2, K3, (P1, K1) twice, P1, K3, P2 **, K1, (P2, K3) 3[4:4:5:5:6] times, P2, K2, rep from ** back to *.

6th row *K2, P6[6:10:10:14:14], K2, P6, K2, P10, K2, P3, (K1, P1) twice, K1, P3, K2 **, (P3, K2) 4[5:5:6:6:7] times, rep from ** back to *.

7th row *(P2, K2) 2[2:3:3:4:4] times, P2, K6, P2, (K2, P2) 3 times, K2, (P1, K1) 3 times, P1, K2, P2 **, P1, (K3, P2) 3[4:4:5:5:6] times, K3, P1, rep from ** back to *.

8th row *(K2, P2) 2[2:3:3:4:4] times, K2, P6, K2, (P2, K2) 3 times, P2, (K1, P1) 3 times, K1, P2, K2, **, (K2, P3) 4[5:5:6:6:7] times, rep from ** back to *.

9th row *P2, K6[6:10:10:14:14], P2, C6B, P2, K10, P2, K1, (P1, K1) 5 times, P2, **, K2, (P2, K3) 3[4:4:5:5:6] times,

Tony Boase

P2, K1, rep from ** back to * but work C6F instead of C6B.

10th row *K2, P6[6:10:10:14:14], K2, P6, K2, P10, K2, P1, (K1, P1) 5 times, K2 ** patt 20[25:25:30:30:35] as 8th row, rep from ** back to *.

11th row Patt 43[43:47:47:51:51] as 7th row, patt 20[25:25:30:30:35] as 7th row, patt to end as 7th row.

12th row Patt 43[43:47:47:51:51] as 8th row, patt 20[25:25:30:30:35] as 6th row, patt to end as 8th row.

13th row Patt 43[43:47:47:51:51] as 5th row, patt 20[25:25:30:30:35] as 5th row, patt to end as 5th row.

14th row Patt 43[43:47:47:51:51] as 6th row, patt 20[25:25:30:30:35] as 4th row, patt to end as 6th row.

15th row Patt 43[43:47:47:51:51] as 3rd row, patt 20[25:25:30:30:35] as 3rd row, patt to end as 3rd row.

16th row Patt 43[43:47:47:51:51] as 4th row, patt 20[25:25:30:30:35] as 2nd row, patt to end as 4th row.
Note that patt over center 20[25:25: 30:30:35] sts repeats over 16 rows, with cables worked on every 6th row; rest of patt is repeated over 16 rows as given. Cont in patt until work measures 24[25:26:26½:27:28]in (61[63:65: 67:69:71]cm) from beg; end with WS row and then start shoulder shaping.

Next row Bind off 22[23:25:27:29:32], K to end.

Next row Bind off 22[23:25:27:29:32], P to end, inc one st on 2nd, 3rd and 6th sizes. 62[66:70:70:74:74] sts.
Change to No. 3 (3¼mm) needles.

Next row K2, *P2, K2, rep from * to end.
Work 6 more rows in ribbing, dec one st at each end of every row. Bind off loosely in ribbing.
Return to sts that were left, sl first 17 sts onto a holder, rejoin yarn and K to end Complete to match back.

Sleeves

Join shoulder seams. Using set of four No. 4 (3¾mm) needles and with RS facing, K across 17 gusset sts, pick up and K 85[90:95:100:105:110] sts around armhole.

1st round Sl1, K1, psso, K13, K2 tog, (P2, K3) to end.

2nd round K15, P1, (K3, P2) to last 4 sts, K3, P1.

3rd round Sl1, K1, psso, K11, K2 tog, (K3, P2) to end.

4th round K15, (P2, K3) to last 3 sts, P2, K1.

5th round Sl1, K1, psso, K9, K2 tog, K1, (P2, K3) to last 4 sts, P2, K2.

6th round K11, (P2, K3) to end.

7th round Sl1, K1, psso, K7, K2 tog, P1, (K3, P2) to last 4 sts, K3, P1.

8th round K9, (K3, P2) to end.

9th round Sl1, K1, psso, K5, K2 tog, K2, P2, (K3, P2) to last st, K1.

10th round K7, patt to end as for 8th round.

11th round Sl1, K1, psso, K3, K2 tog, patt to end as 7th round.

12th round K5, patt to end as 6th round.

13th round Sl1, K1, psso, K1, K2 tog, patt to end as 5th round.

14th round K5, patt to end as 4th round.

15th round Sl1, K2 tog, psso, patt to end as 3rd round. 86[91:96:101:106: 111] sts.

16th round K1, patt to end as 2nd round.

17th round K1, patt to end as first round.

18th round K to end.

19th round P to end.
Rep 18th and 19th rounds once more.

22nd round P1, K to end.

23rd round K to end.
Rep last 2 rounds throughout, dec one st on each side of seam st on next and every foll 6th round (i.e. P1, sl1, K1, psso, K to last 2 sts, K2 tog) until 48[51:54:57:60:63] sts rem. Cont straight until sleeve seam measures 15½[16:16½:17:17½:18]in (40[41:42: 43:44:45]cm); stop at end of round and inc one st at end of last round on 2nd and 6th sizes, dec 2 sts on 3rd size and dec one st on 4th size. 48[52:52:56:60:64] sts. Change to four No. 3 (3¼mm) needles. Work K2, P2 ribbing for 2½in (6cm). Bind off loosely in ribbing.

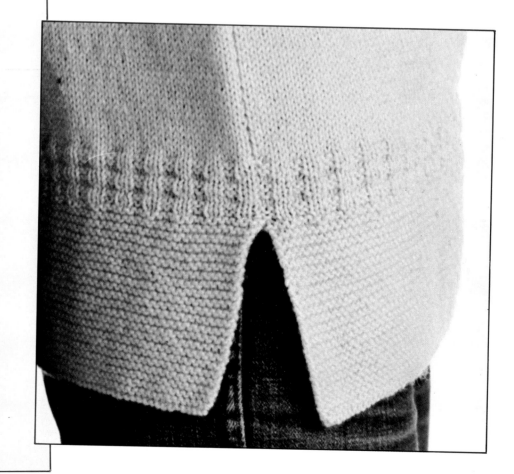

*Traditional Fair Isle
*Carrying and linking in
  yarn
*Weaving yarn across
  fabric
*Stitch Wise: Fair Isle border
  patterns
*Pattern for a woman's
  cardigan

Traditional Fair Isle

Fair Isle knitting originated in one of the Shetland Isles to the north of Scotland. Fair Isle patterns are known for their subtle color combinations, usually soft reds, blues and yellows worked on a natural colored background.

The designs can be worked in narrow or broad bands as a border or they can form an overall pattern.

Although a Fair Isle design may contain many colors, true Fair Isle uses only two colors in a row, the first forming the background fabric and the second the pattern. Because the yarn not in use is carried across the back of the work, a strong double fabric is formed. So that the yarns do not get tangled, one color should be held in your right hand and one color in your left hand (see Volume 3, pages 27-28). Carry the second ball of yarn across the back of the fabric, using it as needed. If the yarn must pass over more than four stitches, it should be woven into the work to avoid leaving long strands and to anchor the stitches in order to prevent them from stretching. during washing or wearing.

Carrying and linking in yarn

It is very important, when working Fair Isle patterns, to carry the yarn not in use evenly across the back of the work. If the yarn is pulled too tight, the fabric will be distorted. When the yarn has to pass over five stitches, it should be linked in at the center of the group so that you do not get long strands across the fabric.

For this sample you will need two colors; A and B.

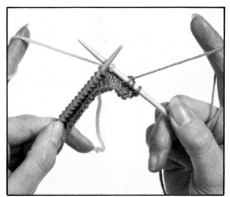

1 With A, cast on 19 stitches and work a few rows. Knit 3 stitches with A, then 1 stitch with B.

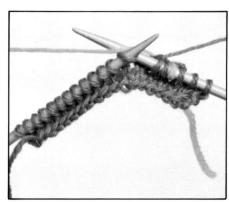

2 The next 5 stitches are worked in A, so B should be linked in on 3rd stitch. With A, knit 2, keeping both colors at back of work. Insert right-hand needle into next stitch in usual way, then take B over right-hand needle.

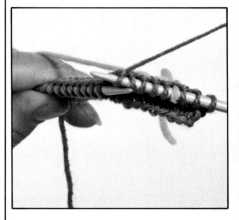

3 Take A around right-hand needle and knit stitch in the usual way. Knit the next 2 stitches with A. Color B has now been linked in at the center of the 5 stitches worked in A.

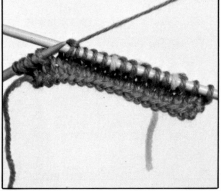

4 Knit the next stitch with B, then repeat steps 2 and 3 over the next 5 stitches.

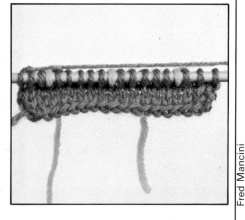

5 Knit the next stitch with B and the last 3 stitches with A. Here, the first row is complete. The 2nd row is worked in the same color as first row. Purl 3 stitches with A, then purl 1 stitch with B.

Fred Mancini

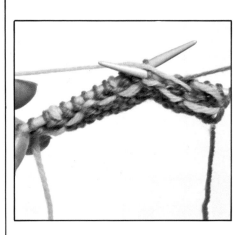

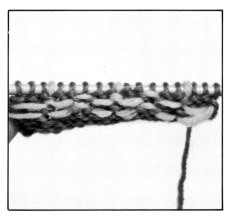

6 The yarn is linked in again over the next group of 5 stitches. With A, purl 2, keeping both colors at front of work. Insert needle into next stitch in the usual way, take B over right-hand needle.

7 Take A around right-hand needle and purl stitch in the usual way. Purl the next 2 stitches with A. Color B has now been linked in at the center of the 5 stitches in A.

8 Purl the next st with B, then repeat steps 6 and 7 over the next 5 stitches. Purl the next stitch with B and the last 3 stitches with A.

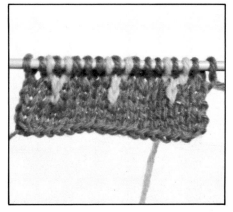

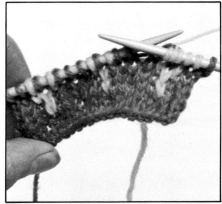

9 On the next 2 rows the yarn doesn't have to be linked in because the largest group of stitches is 3. To work the 3rd row knit 2 A, 1 B, 1 A, 1 B, then work 3 A, 1 B, 1 A, 1 B twice over next 12 stitches, knit the last 2 stitches with A.

10 The 4th row is worked in the same color sequence as the 3rd row but the stitches are purled instead of knitted.

11 The 5th and 6th rows have groups of 5 stitches so the yarn has to be linked in. Knit the first stitch with A, then knit 2 stitches with B, link A in with the next stitch by inserting right-hand needle into the next stitch, then take A over right-hand needle, with B knit stitch in the usual way. Knit 2 stitches with B.

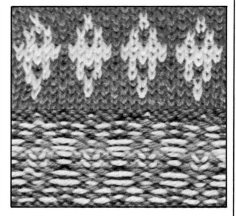

12 Continue to work 1 stitch in A and 5 stitches in B, linking in A as before, to last stitch, knit last st with A. The first half of the pattern is now complete.

13 Now work the pattern rows in reverse order, beginning by purling the first row and following color sequence of last row. This completes one pattern repeat.

14 Here a series of pattern repeats has been worked. The fabric is neat on the right side and the yarn is stranded and linked in evenly on the wrong side.

Fred Mancini

Weaving yarn across fabric

When a large number of stitches in each color is worked, the yarn being carried across the row should be woven in. The yarn is woven in on every other stitch being worked in the first color, which is done by passing the color not in use over the top of the right-hand needle, just as for linking in. This will produce a firm, neat fabric which is ideal for jackets and coats.

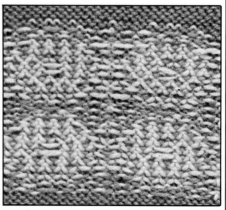

1 This sample shows the right side of the fabric with a large number of stitches worked in each color.

2 This is the wrong side of the same sample. The yarn is woven neatly into every other stitch.

Stitch Wise

Two traditional Fair Isle border patterns

Use 6 colors; A, B, C, D, E and F.
Cast on a multiple of 18 plus 1 extra.
1st row K *3A, 1B, (5A, 1B) twice, 2A, rep from * to last st, 1A.
2nd row P1A, *1A, 2B, 4A, 3B, 4A, 2B, 2A, rep from * to end.
3rd row K *1A, 3B, 5A, 1B, 5A, 3B, rep from * to last st, 1A.
4th row P1C, *2B, 2C, 3B, 3C, 3B, 2C, 2B, 1C, rep from * to end.
5th row K *1C, 1B, 2C, 3B, 5C, 3B, 2C, 1B, rep from * to last st, 1C.
6th row P1E, *2D, 3E, 3D, 1E, 3D, 3E, 2D, 1E, rep from * to end.
7th row K *1F, 2E, 5F, 3E, 5F, 2E, rep from * to last st, 1F.
8th-13th rows As 6th-1st in this order.

For this pattern you will need 3 colors; A, B and C.
Cast on a multiple of 18 plus 1 extra.
1st row K *1B, 1A, 1B, (6A, 1B) twice, 1A, rep from * to last st, 1B.
2nd row P1B, *1B, 1A, 1B, 4A, 3B, 4A, 1B, 1A, 2B, rep from * to end.
3rd row K *1B, 3A, 1B, 2A, 2B, 1A, 2B, 2A, 1B, 3A, rep from * to last st, 1B.
4th row P1B, *4A, 1B, 1A, 5B, 1A, 1B, 4A, 1B, rep from * to end.
5th row K *1A, 1B, 4A, 3B, 1A, 3B, 4A, 1B, rep from * to end.
6th row P1C, *3A, 3C, 2A, 1C, 2A, 3C, 3A, 1C, rep from * to end.
7th row K * 3A, 4C, 1A, (1C, 1A) twice, 4C, 2A, rep from * to last st, 1A.
8th row P1A, *1A, 2C, 1A, (1C, 1A) 5 times, 2C, 2A, rep from * to end.
9th-15th rows Work 7th-1st rows in this order.

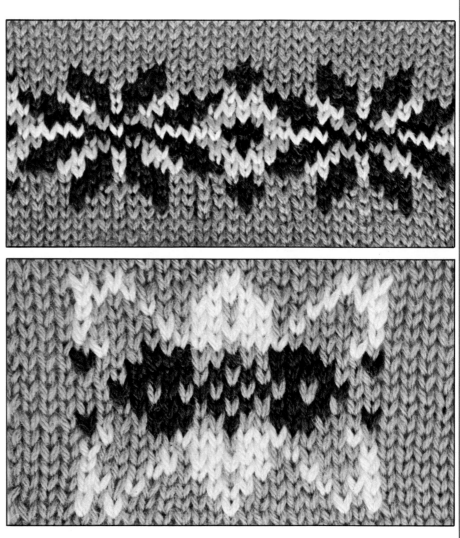

One pattern repeat only is shown here.

Fred Mancini

Fair Isle cardigan

Bands of Fair Isle patterning make this classic cardigan something you'll never get tired of wearing. We have worked it in pale shades but choose brighter colors for a bold look.

Sizes
To fit 32[34:36:38:40]in (83[87:92:97:102]cm) bust.
Length, 22½[23:23½:24:24½]in (57[58:59:60:61]cm).
Sleeve seam, 17[17½:17¾:18:18½]in (43[44:45:46:47]cm).

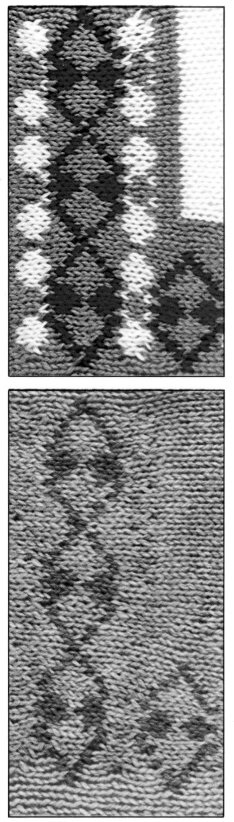

Note Directions for larger sizes are in brackets [ ]; where there is only one set of figures it applies to all sizes.

Materials

- 5[6:6:7:8] x 2oz (50g) balls of knitting worsted in main color (A)
- 2[2:2:3:3] balls in contrasting color (B)
- 1[1:1:2:2] balls in contrasting color (C)
- 1 pair each Nos. 3 and 5 (3¼ and 4mm) knitting needles
- Nos. 3 and 5 (3¼ and 4mm) circular needles
- 5 buttons

Gauge

22 sts and 30 rows to 4in (10cm) in stockinette st on No. 5 (4mm) needles.

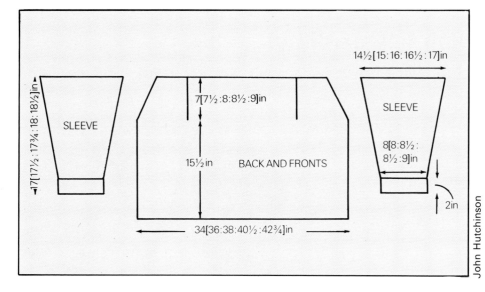

14½[15:16:16½:17]in

SLEEVE

17[17½:17¾:18:18½]in

SLEEVE

8[8:8½:8½:9]in

7[7½:8:8½:9]in

15½ in   BACK AND FRONTS

2in

34[36:38:40½:42¾]in

John Hutchinson

Back and fronts

Using No. 5 (4mm) needles and A, cast on 25 sts for pocket lining. Beg with a K row, work 24 rows stockinette st. Cut off yarn and leave sts on holder. Make another lining in same way. Using No. 3 (3¼mm) circular needle and A, cast on 187[199:211:223:235] sts and work in one piece to underarm.

1st row P1, *K1, P1, rep from * to end.
2nd row K1, *P1, K1, rep from * to end.
Rep these 2 rows for 3in (8cm); end with 2nd row. With No. 5 (4mm) circular needle cont in stockinette st, working border patt as foll:
1st row Using B, K to end.
2nd row Using B, P to end.
3rd row As first.
4th row P5 B, *2 A, 5 B, 2 A, 3 B, rep from * to last 2 sts, 2 B.
5th row K4 B, *4 A, 3 B, 4 A, 1 B, rep from * to last 3 sts, 3 B.
6th row As 5th, but P instead of K.
7th row K5 B, *2A, (1 B, 1 A) twice, 1 B, 2 A, 3 B, rep from * to last 2 sts, 2 B.
8th row P7 B, *(1 C, 1 B) 3 times, 6 B, rep from * to end.
9th row K6 B, *1 C, 1 B, 3 C, 1 B, 1 C, 5 B, rep from * to last st, 1 B.
10th row P5 B, *1 C, 2 B, 3 C, 2 B, 1 C, 3 B, rep from * to last 2 sts, 2 B.
11th row K4 B, *(1 C, 4 B) twice, 1 C, 1 B, rep from * to last 3 sts, 3 B.
12th row P3 B, *1 C, 11 B, rep from * to last 4 sts, 1 C, 3 B.
13th-19th rows Work as 11th-5th in this order.
20th row Patt 11 as 7th but P; patt as 4th to last 11 sts; patt 11 as 7th but P.
21st row K7 B, (1 C, 1 B) twice, 1 C, work in B to last 12 sts, join in a second ball of C, work (1 C, 1 B) twice, 1 C, 7 B.
22nd row P6 B, 1 C, 1 B, 3 C, 1 B, 1 C, work in B to last 13 sts, 1 C, 1 B, 3 C, 1 B, 1 C, 6 B.
23rd row K5 B, 1 C, 2 B, 3 C, 2 B, 1 C, work in B to last 14 sts, 1 C, 2 B, 3 C, 2 B, 1 C, 5 B.
24th row (P4 B, 1 C) 3 times, 3 B, join

in A, using A, P to last 18 sts, P3 B, (1 C, 4 B) 3 times.
25th row K3B, 1 C, 11 B, 1 C, 2 B, sl next 25 sts onto holder for pocket top, K across sts of pocket lining, using A, K to last 43 sts, sl next 25 sts onto holder, K across sts of pocket lining, K2B, 1 C, 11 B, 1 C, B 3.
Keeping 18 sts at each end in patt as now set and rem sts in A, cont until work measures 15½in (39cm) from beg, ending with a K row.

Divide for armholes

Next row Keeping patt at front edge correct, P47[50:53:56:59], turn. Cont on these sts for left front.
Next row K to last 20 sts, K2 tog, patt to end. Work 2 rows.
Next row Patt 18, P2 tog, P to end. Cont to dec on every 3rd row as shown until 28[30:32:34:36] sts rem. Cont without shaping until armhole measures 7[7½:8:8½:9]in (18[19:20:21:22]cm) from beg, ending with a P row. Leave sts on a holder for grafting.
With WS of work facing, rejoin A to sts that were left, P93[99:105:111:117] sts, turn. Cont on these sts for back until armholes measure same as front, ending with a P row.
Next row Sl first 28[30:32:34:36] sts onto holder, bind off center 37[39:41:43:45] sts and cut off yarn, sl rem sts onto another holder.
With WS of work facing, rejoin yarn to rem sts, P to last 18 sts, patt 18.
Next row Patt 18, sl 1, K1, psso, K to end.
Next row P to last 20 sts, P2 tog tbl, patt to end. Complete to match left front.

Sleeves

Using No. 3 (3¼mm) needles and A, cast on 45[45:47:47:49] sts. Rib 2in (5cm) as for back and fronts; end with 2nd row. With No. 5 (4mm) needles cont in stockinette st, work 3 rows using B.
4th row P1[1:2:2:3] B, *2 A, 3 B, 2 A, 5 B, rep from * twice more, 2 A, 3 B,

2 A, 1[1:2:2:3] B.
5th row K0[0:1:1:2] B, *4 A, 1 B, 4 A, 3 B, rep from * twice more, 4 A, 1 B, 0[0:1:1:2] B.
6th row As 5th, but P instead of K.
7th row K1[1:2:2:3] B, *2 A, 3 B, 2 A, (1 B, 1 A) twice, 1 B, rep from * twice more, 2 A, 3 B, 2 A, 1[1:2:2:3] B.
Cont in patt as set to match border on bodice until 20 rows have been worked in stockinette st. Work 3 more rows using B, inc 2[4:4:6:6] sts evenly across last row. 47[49:51:53:55] sts.
Beg with a P row, cont in stockinette st using A, inc one st at each end of 2nd and every foll 5th row until there are 79[83:87:91:95] sts. Cont straight until sleeve measures 17[17½:17¾:18:18½]in (43[44:45:46:47]cm); end with P row. Bind off loosely.

Front band

Graft shoulder sts tog. Using No. 3 (3¼mm) needles and A, cast on 11 sts. Rib 1½in (4cm) as for back and fronts, ending with a 2nd row.
Next row (buttonhole row) Rib 4, bind off 3, rib to end.
Next row Rib to end, casting on 3 sts over those bound off in previous row. Cont in ribbing, making 4 more buttonholes at intervals of approx 2¾in (7cm), until band fits up front edge, around back neck and down other front. Bind off.

Pocket tops

Sl 25 sts onto No. 3 (3¼mm) needle; using A and with RS of work facing, (P1, K1) into first st, (P1, K1) to last 2 sts, P1, (K1, P1) into last st. 27 sts. Rib 1in (3cm). Bind off in ribbing.

To finish

Press or block according to yarn used. Join sleeve seams. Set in sleeves. Sew down pocket linings and ends of pocket tops. Sew front band in place and add buttons.

*Working Fair Isle from a chart
*Repeating a Fair Isle pattern
*Stitch Wise: more Fair Isle patterns
*Patterns for two Fair Isle sweaters

Working Fair Isle from a chart

Fair Isle patterns can be shown either in written form or in chart form. Many patterns are very long when given as row-by-row directions so it is easier and more concise to chart the pattern. This not only makes the instructions shorter, it also gives you a good idea of what the finished pattern will look like. There are two kinds of chart, one that shows each stitch in a color and one in which each stitch is represented by a symbol. Each square on a chart represents one stitch and each horizontal line of squares a row of knitting. The chart shows the right side of the knitting; the odd-numbered (RS) rows are read from right to left, and the even-numbered (WS) rows are read from left to right.

1 This chart shows each stitch in color. If you use different colors from the ones shown here, remember which colors you have changed and carry these colors all the way through.

2 This is the same chart showing how different it looks when symbols are used. In the key, each letter represents a color; that is, A=blue, B=pink, C=yellow, D=green, E=purple and F=beige. You can select your own colors and substitute them for the symbols.

3 This is the finished sample using the colors shown on the colored chart. The key for the chart with symbols will be X = A (blue), O = B (pink), − = C (yellow), ● = D (green), ■ = E (purple), □ = F (beige).

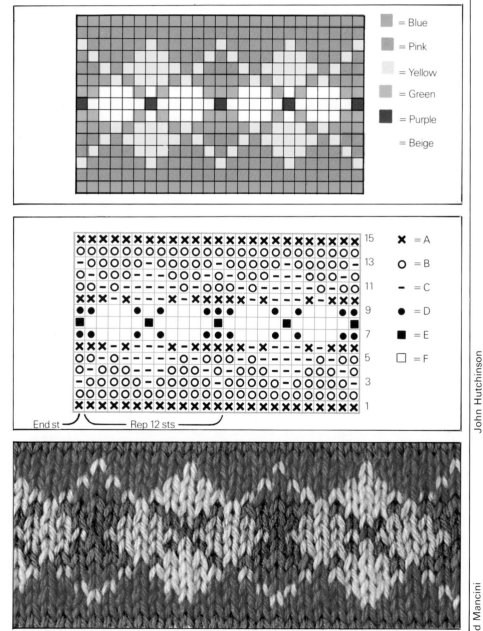

= Blue
= Pink
= Yellow
= Green
= Purple
= Beige

15
13
11
9
7
5
3
1

✗ = A
O = B
− = C
● = D
■ = E
□ = F

End st — Rep 12 sts

John Hutchinson

Fred Mancini

Repeating a Fair Isle pattern

Pattern directions will tell you how many stitches to cast on for each section of a garment and the Fair Isle pattern will repeat across this number of stitches, but if you want to work out a Fair Isle pattern of your own design, you will need to know the pattern repeat. Most Fair Isle samples give you the number of stitches in each repeat plus the number you need for the end.

For the sample shown here you need a multiple of 12 plus 1 extra. Cast on a multiple of 12 (24, 36, 48 etc), then cast on an extra stitch to balance the repeat.

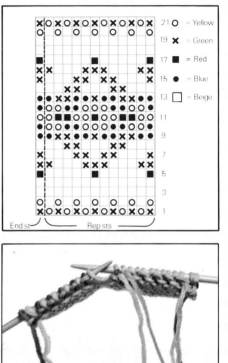

21 O = Yellow
19 X = Green
17 ■ = Red
15 ● = Blue
13 □ = Beige

End st ⌐ Rep sts

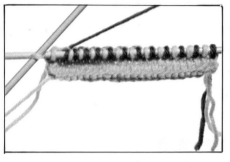

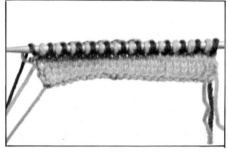

1 Cast on 25 stitches. Work the first row from the right-hand edge to the dotted line on the chart. Do not work the stitch beyond the line at this stage but repeat the first 12 stitches once more.

2 One stitch remains on left-hand needle: this is the end stitch that will balance the pattern. Following the chart, pattern the last stitch.

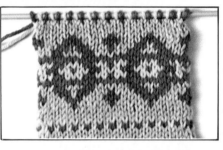

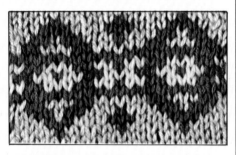

3 On the second and all following WS rows, work to the dotted line, then repeat from the dotted line to the end of the chart twice.

4 Continue to work from the chart until the 21st row has been completed. This completes one repeat of the chart.

5 This Fair Isle pattern can be used as an overall pattern by omitting the border lines (rows 1, 2, 3 and 4 and rows 17, 18, 19, 20 and 21) on each side of the main pattern. This sample shows two repeats in width and 1 repeat in depth with the border lines omitted.

Stitch Wise

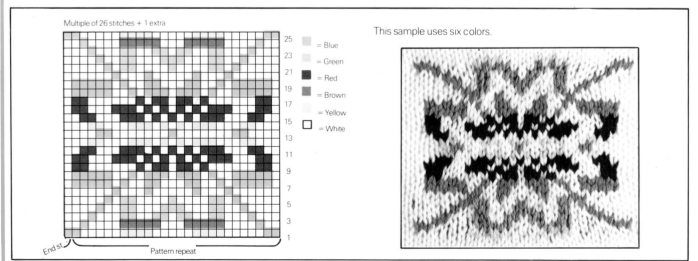

Multiple of 26 stitches + 1 extra

25
23
21
19
17
15
13
11
9
7
5
3
1

□ = Blue
□ = Green
■ = Red
■ = Brown
□ = Yellow
□ = White

End st. ⌐ Pattern repeat

This sample uses six colors.

Fred Mancini

John Hutchinson

Fair Isle sweaters

Fair Isle patterns enhance these classic sweaters.

Sizes

To fit 30[32:34:36]in (76[83:87:92]cm)
Length, 23[23:24:24]in (58[58:61:61]cm).
Sweater sleeve seam, 16[16:17:17]in (40[40:43:43]cm).
Note Directions for larger sizes are in brackets []; where there is only one set of figures it applies to all sizes.

Materials

Knitting worsted
Sweater with sleeves
   14[15:15:16] × 1oz (25g) balls in main shade (A)
   3[3:3:4] balls in contrasting color (B)
   Sleeveless sweater *5[5:5:6] × 1oz (25g) balls in main shade (A)*
   3[3:4:4] balls in contrasting color (B)
   3[3:3:4] balls in contrasting color (C)
   2[2:2:3] balls in contrasting color (D)
   2 balls in contrasting color (E)
   1 pair each Nos. 3 and 5 (3¼ and 4mm) knitting needles

Gauge

22 sts and 28 rows to 4in (10cm) in stockinette st on No. 5 (4mm) needles.

Sweater with sleeves

Back

Using No. 3 (3¼mm) needles and A, cast

Victor Yuan

on 94[100:106:112] sts. Work 2¼in (6cm) K1, P1 ribbing. Change to No. 5 (4mm) needles. Beg with a K row, cont in stockinette st until work measures

15[15:16:16]in (38[38:41:41]cm); end with P row.
Shape armholes
Bind off 9[10:11:12] sts at beg of next

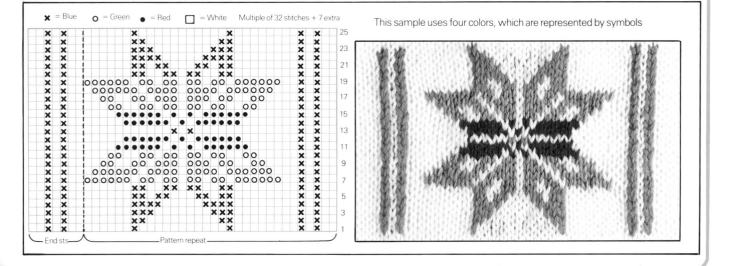

× = Blue   o = Green   ● = Red   ☐ = White   Multiple of 32 stitches + 7 extra

This sample uses four colors, which are represented by symbols

End sts   Pattern repeat

2 rows. 76[80:84:88] sts. ** Cont
straight until work measures 23[23:24:
24]in (58[58:61:61]cm); end with P
row.

Shape shoulders

Bind off 8[9:9:9] sts at beg of next 4
rows and 9[8:9:10] sts at beg of foll 2
rows. Bind off rem 26[28:30:32] sts.

Front

Using No. 3 (3¼mm) needles and A, cast
on 94[100:106:112] sts. Work 2¼in
(6cm) K1, P1 ribbing, inc one st at end of
last row on 1st and 2nd sizes and dec one
st at end of last row on 3rd and 4th sizes.
95[101:105:111] sts. Change to No. 5
(4mm) needles. Beg with a K row, cont in
stockinette st and work in patt from chart
A until work measures 15[15:16:16] in
(38[38:41:41]cm); end with P row.

Shape armholes and divide for neck

Bind off 9[10:11:12] sts at beg of next
2 rows. 77[81:83:87] sts.
Next row Patt 36[38:39:41] sts, K2
tog, turn.
Complete left side of neck first. Dec one
st at neck edge on every 3rd row until
25[26:27:28] sts rem. Cont without
shaping until work measures same as
back to shoulder, end with P row.

Shape shoulder

Bind off 8[9:9:9] sts at beg of next and
foll alternate row. Work one row. Bind off
rem 9[8:9:10] sts. With RS of work facing,
return to rem sts, sl first st onto a safety
pin, rejoin yarn to next st and patt to end
of row. Complete to match first side,
reversing all shaping.

Sleeves

Using No. 3 (3¼mm) needles and A, cast
on 60[62:64:66] sts. Work 3in (8cm)
K1, P1 ribbing. Change to No. 5 (4mm)
needles. Beg with a K row, cont in
stockinette st, inc one st at each end of
3rd and every foll 6th row until there

are 88 sts. Cont without shaping until
work measures 17[17:18:18]in (43[43:
46:46]cm); end with P row. Bind off.

Neckband

Join right shoulder seam. Using No. 3 (3¼
mm) needles, A and with RS of work
facing, pick up and K 59 sts down left
side of neck, K one st from safety pin,
pick up and K 59 sts up right side of neck
and 26[28:30:32] sts across back.
145[147:149:151] sts.
1st row K1, (P1, K1) 41 [42:43:44]
times, P2 tog tbl, P1, P2 tog, rib to end.
2nd row (P1, K1) 27 times, P1, K2
tog, K1, sl 1, K1, psso, rib to end.
Rib 4 more rows, dec in same way at
each side of center front st. Bind off
loosely in ribbing.

To finish

Press or block, according to yarn used.
Join left shoulder and neckband seam.
Sew sleeves in position, placing 1in
(3cm) of row ends at top of sleeve to
bound-off sts at underarm. Join side and
sleeve seams. Press seams.

CHART A ☐ = A ○ = B

Repeat 10 sts.

CHART B ╱ = A ○ = B ☐ = C ✕ = D ■ = E

Repeat 6 sts

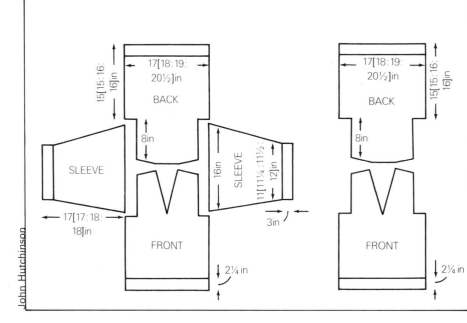

Sleeveless sweater

Back
Work as for sweater back, working in patt from chart B after completing waistband.

Front
Work as for sweater back to **.
Divide for neck

Next row Patt 36[38:40:42] sts, K2 tog, turn.
Cont in patt on these sts as for left side of sweater front. Rejoin yarn to rem sts and work to match first side, reversing shaping.

Neckband
Work as for sweater, but pick up and K one st at center front.

Armbands
Join left shoulder and neckband seams. Using No. 3 (3¼mm) needles, A and with RS facing, pick up and K 120 sts evenly around armhole. Work 6 rows K1, P1 ribbing. Bind off loosely in ribbing.

To finish
Press or block, according to yarn used. Join side seams. Press seams.

Victor Yuan

49

Sewing / COURSE 38

* Working with lace fabrics
* Tucks
* Wedding gown:
  adapting the pattern
  directions for making

Working with lace fabrics

Lace fabrics are available in cotton, rayon, wool, linen, silk and other fibers, and they vary in price according to their composition and to whether they are hand or machine made.

They can be used for edgings, insertions, or to make an entire garment, and they add a delicate touch to women's and children's blouses and dresses, babies' clothes, and lingerie.

Because of the delicate network of threads in lace, special care is needed when cutting out and sewing.

1 Transfer the markings from the pattern to the fabric using tailor's tacks.
If the lace fabric has a one-way design, lay the pattern pieces on the fabric in one direction only. Use sharp, fine pins and pin within the seam allowance only. Baste all seams before sewing to prevent slipping.

2 The design of the pattern in the lace must be matched where possible and should always be matched carefully if the seam falls in a visible position.
Use either French seams or double stitched seams (see Volume 7, page 76) working with a thread appropriate to the fabric and using a short stitch, and fine needle.

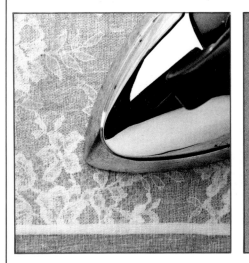

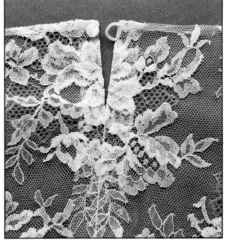

3 Use a damp cloth when pressing and always press from the wrong side, with a terrycloth or wool press pad under the fabric. This prevents the surface of the lace from being flattened.

4 Instead of using facings, which would spoil the finished effect of the lace, you can bias-bind raw edges with satin, taffeta or organza in a color matching the lace, or hem the edges with a very fine slip stitch.

5 Use a lightweight zipper if this type of fastening is required. Insert it into the garment using the slot seam method shown in Volume 4, page 68 and sew it in by hand.
If buttons are used, choose small buttons and use thread loops to fasten them.

Paul Williams

Tucks

Tucks are stitched folds on the right side of a garment which are used either for decoration or to add shaping. When the tucks are used for shaping they usually fall only part of the way down the garment so that the release at the base of the tuck adds fullness. For this reason they are often called released tucks.

Tucks should always be worked on the straight grain of the fabric. They can vary in width—the narrowest pin tucks can measure as little as $\frac{1}{8}$in (3mm) from the stitching line to the fold. Wider tucks can be anything up to $\frac{3}{4}$in (2cm) wide.

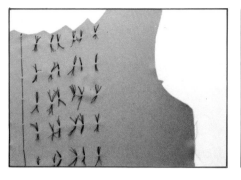

1 If the tuck lines are marked on the pattern, transfer them to the fabric with lines of tailor's tacks.

2 Fold the fabric with wrong sides together so that the tailor's tacks are even. Baste the two layers together on the stitching line, the width of the tuck from the fold. Stitch along the line of basting. Press the tuck in the direction indicated on the pattern. Secure the thread ends on the wrong side.

Making your own tucks

1 If tucks are not included on the pattern, decide how many tucks you wish to make, how wide they should be and the spacing between each tuck. Calculate how much extra fabric this will require.
Cut out a rectangle of fabric which will accommodate the pattern and the area to be tucked.

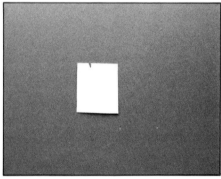

2 Make a cardboard gauge to help form the tucks. Measure the width of the tuck from the left-hand edge of the cardboard, and cut a notch at this point. Then the distance from the notch to the right-hand edge should be the space between the tucks.

3 Mark the first two tuck lines on the fabric by measuring out from the straight edge with a tapemeasure. Mark the position of the tuck lines every 2in (5cm) down the fabric to keep them straight. Baste and stitch. Press the tuck away from the center of the garment.

4 Match the right-hand edge of the gauge to the stitching line of the first tuck. Fold the fabric level with the left-hand edge of the gauge and baste the tuck in place level with the notch.

5 Stitch the tuck from the wrong side and press. Stitch the remaining tucks in the same way, pressing them all outward.

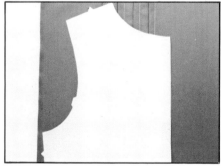

6 Place the pattern piece on the fabric with the tucks in the correct position, making sure that they do not overlap any darts. Pin in place and cut out. The garment is now completed in the usual way.

Paul Williams

Jean Claude Volpeliere

Wedding gown

Measurements

The wedding gown is made by adapting the pattern for the dress from the Stitch by Stitch Pattern Pack, available in sizes 10 to 20, corresponding to sizes 8 to 18 in ready-made clothes. Alterations include $\frac{5}{8}$in (1.5cm) seam allowances unless otherwise stated.

Adapting the pattern

Materials

Three sheets of tracing paper at least 24 x 65in (60 x 165cm)
Cellophane tape
Ruler or yardstick; flexible curve

1 Trace the front and back dress pattern pieces leaving enough paper at the lower edges to extend the pattern.

2 Decide on the finished dress length by measuring from the back neck. Using a yardstick extend the dress side seams; center front and center back line to the finished length required. Draw in the hemline by measuring down at intervals from original hemline on both pieces. Add a 2½in (6.5cm) hem allowance.

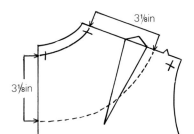

3 Measure down 3⅛in (8cm) from neck seamline at center back and mark this point. Measure 3⅛in (8cm) along shoulder seamline from neck seam line and mark this point. Connect points with a flexible curve for yoke line, keeping line 3⅛in (8cm) from neck.

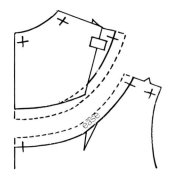

4 Cut along the back on the yoke line. Close the shoulder dart on the yoke and tape in place. Using a flexible curve, reshape the lower edge of the yoke at the bottom of the dart. Tape paper under the patterns and add a ⅜in (1cm) seam allowance to curved edge of yoke and yoke edge of dress. The bottom of the dart on the main back piece is ignored as this edge will be eased into yoke seam.

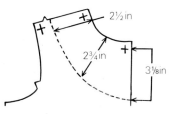

5 Mark a point 3⅛in (8cm) down from neck seamline at center front and mark a second point 2½in (6.5cm) from neck seamline at shoulder. Mark a third point 2¾in (7cm) out from neck seamline half way between these two points. Join the three points with a flexible curve to form the yoke line.

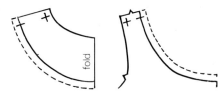

6 Cut the pattern along the yoke line and tape paper under both pieces. Add a ⅜in (1cm) seam allowance to curved edge of both yoke and dress.

7 To allow for the tucks, draw a line 1¾in (4.5cm) out from, and parallel to, center front, extending down to hem. Draw a line ¼in (6mm) in from new center front edge to mark first tuck line. Mark bottom of tuck 6¼in (16cm) from yoke seamline. Draw three more tucks ½in (1.2cm) wide with ¾in (2cm) intervals between each. The depth of these three tucks should be 5½in, 4½in and 3½in (14, 11.5, 9cm) respectively, working from the center out. Ignore waist darts on dress front and back.

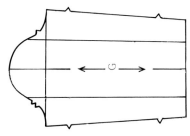

8 Trace the sleeve pattern. Draw a line across the sleeve by joining the tops of the side seams. Extend the grain line to both edges of the sleeve. Draw new side seamlines parallel to the grain line from the top edges of the original side seams. Add two more lines, half way between the grain line and the seamlines, first measuring along the upper horizontal line and the lower edge and then connecting the points as shown.

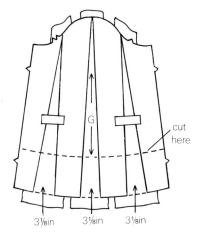

9 Slash along these lines from lower sleeve edge to top of sleeve cap. Open each slash 3⅛in (8cm) at lower edge and tape paper underneath. Mark the grain line through the center of the sleeve. Since the lower sleeve is finished in lace, the pattern is shortened. Measure up 6in (15cm) from lower sleeve edge at intervals and join the points to form the new sleeve edge.

10 For the pattern for the lace at the end of the sleeve, lay tracing paper over the lower part of the enlarged sleeve pattern. Trace the new seamline and draw in a new cutting line ⅝in (1.5cm) above it. Trace side cutting lines and the original cutting line around the lower edge of the sleeve to give a gently curved pattern piece ⅝in (1.5cm) seam allowances are already included on the pattern piece.

Terry Evans

Directions for making (1)

Suggested fabrics
Soft, drapeable fabrics such as crepe, crepe de chine, satin-finish rayon.

Materials
45in (115cm)- wide fabric with or
   without nap:
   Sizes 10, 12 and 14: $4\frac{7}{8}$yd (4.4m)
   Sizes 16, 18 and 20: $5\frac{1}{8}$yd (4.6m)
36in (90cm)- wide lace fabric with
   scalloped edge with/without one-
   way design:
   For all sizes: $1\frac{7}{8}$yd (1.7m)
1in (2.5cm)- wide lace:
   Sizes 10, 12 and 14: $\frac{3}{4}$yd (.7m)
   Sizes 16, 18 and 20: $\frac{7}{8}$yd (.8m)
Matching sewing thread
18in (46cm) dress zipper
Three $\frac{1}{4}$in (6mm)- diameter buttons
$\frac{3}{4}$yd (.6m) of $\frac{1}{4}$in (6mm) ribbon
3yd (2.8m) of $\frac{1}{2}$in (1.2cm) ribbon
Silk thread for tassels, hook and eye

1 Alter the pattern pieces for the dress as shown on page 53.
2 Prepare the two fabrics and pin on the pattern pieces as shown in the layouts. From the remaining main fabric, cut four bias strips $1\frac{3}{8}$in (3.5cm) wide and $27\frac{1}{2}$in (70cm) long for the tie belt.
3 Transfer all markings from the pattern pieces to the fabric.
4 Staystitch around the curved edges of the front and back yokes on the seamline, $\frac{3}{8}$in (1cm) from the raw edge.
5 Fold, baste and stitch the bust darts and press them downward.
6 Fold, baste and stitch the tucks in the front of the dress as shown on page 51 starting from the center and working outward. Press the center tuck toward the left and the tucks on each side outward.
7 Baste and stitch the center back seam to within 18in (46cm) of the yoke seamline with right sides together and notches matching. Finish the seam allowances and press open.

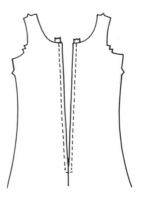

8 Insert the zipper into the center back opening using the slot seam method shown in Volume 4, page 68 with the top of the zipper at the yoke seamline.

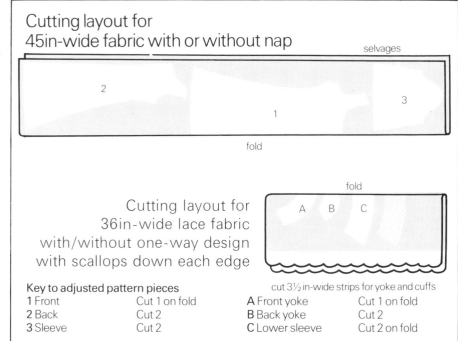

Cutting layout for 45in-wide fabric with or without nap

selvages

2

1

3

fold

Cutting layout for 36in-wide lace fabric with/without one-way design with scallops down each edge

fold

A B C

cut 3½ in-wide strips for yoke and cuffs

Key to adjusted pattern pieces
1 Front	Cut 1 on fold	A Front yoke	Cut 1 on fold
2 Back	Cut 2	B Back yoke	Cut 2
3 Sleeve	Cut 2	C Lower sleeve	Cut 2 on fold

John Hutchinson

9 Baste and stitch the shoulder seams of the dress with right sides together and notches matching. Finish the seam allowances and press open.

10 Baste and stitch the shoulder seams of the yoke with French seams. Press them toward the back.

11 Cut two 23½in (60cm) lengths of scalloped edging for the cuffs and put them aside. Cut one 43½in (110cm) strip and two 14in (35cm) strips for trimming yoke of dress. Join the two shorter pieces to the longer piece using French seams.

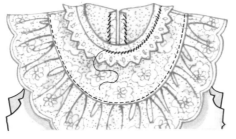

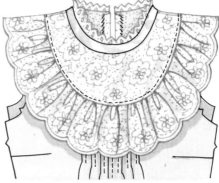

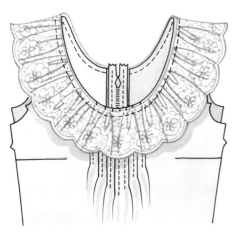

12 Turn under and baste a ⅜in (1cm) seam allowance around the curved edge of the yoke. Press.
Run a line of gathering stitches around the straight edge of the ruffle and draw it up to fit dress.
Pin the lace around yoke edge of the dress with the wrong side of the lace to the right side of the fabric and the edges together. Pin and baste, making sure that the gathers are evenly distributed.

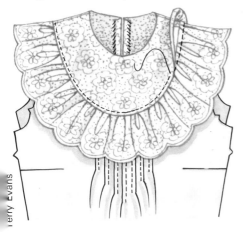

13 Lap edge of the yoke ⅜in (1cm) over edge of the dress yoke seam with raw edges of the lace between the layers.
Pin and baste in place, easing the dress into the yoke at the back curves.
Topstitch the yoke in place close to the folded edge. Press. Trim raw edges to ¼in (6mm) and overcast by hand to finish.
Finish edges of yoke and ruffles.

14 Gather the 1in (2.5cm)-wide lace to fit around the neck edge of the yoke. Pin edging to the yoke ⅝in (1.5cm) from raw edge, with right sides together. Working from right to left, sew the edging to the yoke with small overcasting stitches. The stitches should be loose, so that the edging can be pressed upward and will lie flat.
Trim seam allowance on yoke neck to ¼in (6mm) and overcast by hand.

15 Cut a piece of ¼in (6mm)-wide ribbon to fit around a neck edge, plus a little extra at each end. Turn in ends and press flat. Place ribbon over neck edging seam and baste in place.
Slip stitch in place along both edges.
Directions concluded in next course.

Jean Claude Volpeliere

Terry Evans

Lace edging for sleeve

This lace edging is made up from a curved strip of lace, about 6in (15cm) deep, which is applied to the curved edge of a shortened sleeve.

The ruffle at the cuff is cut from a strip of scalloped lace. The seams are trimmed with strips of ribbon, with an extra band for a decorative touch, and the cuff is fastened at the wrist with a button and thread loop.

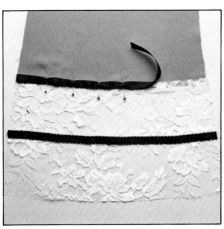

1 Trim the seam allowance at the lower edge of unseamed sleeve to $\frac{1}{4}$in (6mm). Overcast remaining seam allowance to finish. Fold down $\frac{5}{8}$in (1.5cm) seam allowance around inner curve of lace section. Pin, baste and stitch in place around lower edge, close to folded edge of lace. Press.

2 Cut two lengths of ribbon to fit around the sleeve. With wrong side of ribbon against right side of lace, pin one length over seamline. Slip stitch along both edges of ribbon. Pin and slip stitch the second length of ribbon along the center of lace.

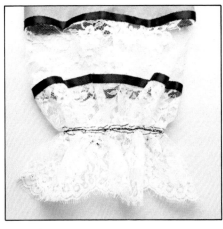

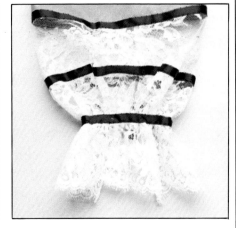

3 Making a French seam, sew underarm sleeve seam to lower band of ribbon. Press seam to back. Clip seam allowance. Fold in $\frac{1}{4}$in (6mm) and a further $\frac{3}{8}$in (1cm) along each side of opening. Slip stitch to lace. Press.

4 Gather the lower edge of sleeve lace to fit wrist. Make a $\frac{1}{8}$in (3mm) double hem at each short end of scalloped strip. Gather straight edge of scalloped strip. Place the gathered edges together with right sides facing and pin. Overcast together.

5 On the right side, conceal the seamline with ribbon, as in step 2 above. Sew on a button and make a button loop for the wrist fastening. Repeat for second sleeve.

Lace insertions in sleeve

Inserting a width of lace into an unseamed sleeve is a good way to add lace trim without adding the extra length of an edging or cuff.

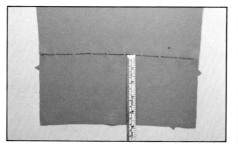

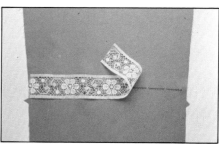

1 Measure the appropriate distance up from the cuff edge of sleeve. Mark a series of dots across the sleeve at this distance and run a line of basting across the sleeve connecting these dots.

2 With wrong side of lace on right side of sleeve, pin and baste the lace, so that the center of lace lies along the basting line.

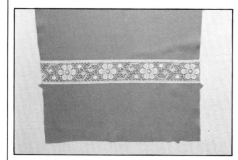

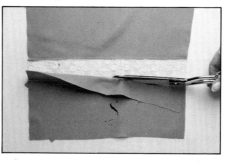

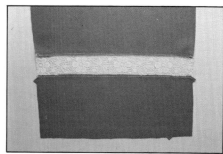

3 Stitch close to the edge of both sides of lace.

4 Turn sleeve inside out. Trim the fabric between stitching lines to within $\frac{1}{8}$in (3mm) of stitching, being careful not to cut the lace.

5 Overcast the raw edges to prevent fraying. Press fabric edges away from the lace.

Silk tassels

Tassels are used as a finish for the ends of a tie belt or cord belt and as a decorative finish to a pointed hood, a scarf or pillows. You can make tassels from almost any yarn, depending on where they are used. For instance, wool would be used for a knitted scarf or shawl, cotton for pillows, and silk for a more delicate finish to a special garment, like the wedding dress shown in this course.

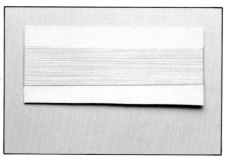

1 Cut a piece of cardboard to desired length for tassel and 2in (5cm) wide. Using silk thread, starting with the end of the thread at bottom of cardboard, wind around cardboard to desired fullness. End with thread at bottom of cardboard.

2 Tie the thread loops together at the top with a length of the same thread, threaded through a needle.
Cut the loops across the bottom and remove the cardboard.

3 Fold the threads over the knot at the top and bind threads together $\frac{5}{8}$in (1.5cm) from the top of tassel.

4 Push the needle up under the binding thread and bring it up at the top.

5 Use this thread to attach the tassel to the end of the belt.

Paul Williams

57

To love, honor and cherish

Here are the directions for completing the wedding gown started on page 54.

Directions for making (2)

4 Sew underarm seam with a French seam, sewing as far as the center ribbon trim.

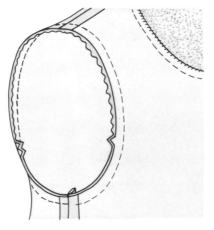

5 Baste and stitch sleeve into armhole with right sides together and the notches matching.

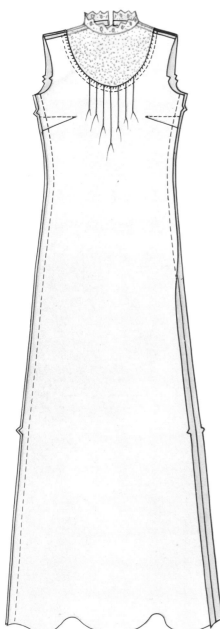

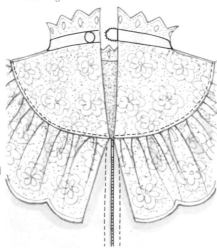

1 With right sides and notches matching, baste and stitch side seams of dress. Finish and press seams open.
2 Finish the lower edge of sleeve and apply lace edging cuff, following directions on page 56. Trim with ribbon as shown.
3 Run two rows of gathering stitches around sleeve cap, between notches. Gather up the sleeve cap to fit armhole.

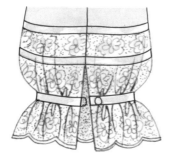

6 Make a thread loop at the left center back neck opening under the edge of ribbon trim. Make thread loops on the back edge of each sleeve opening, at wrist. Sew buttons onto the opposite sides under loops.

7 Join the bias strips together for the belt. Make the strip into a tube as shown in Volume 1, page 57. Following directions on page 57, make two silk tassels and sew to the ends of the belt.

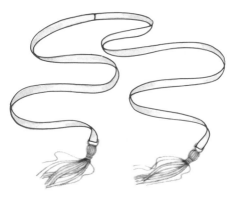

8 Try the dress on with the belt tied in place and mark hemline. Turn the hem up and baste, close to the folded edge. Trim hem to an even depth if necessary. Finish the raw edge of hem by overcasting and sew to dress with invisible hemming. Remove the basting and press the folded edge only.

Jean Claude Volpeliere

Terry Evans

Sewing / COURSE 40

Shoulder pads

Shoulder pads are used either to emphasize the shoulder line in a garment or to correct figure faults such as badly sloping or uneven shoulders. They are most often found in tailored coats and jackets but can also be used in blouses, dresses and unlined jackets. When shoulder pads are used in blouses and dresses, they are usually covered in the same fabric as the garment itself. In suits and coats, however, this is unnecessary as the pad is hidden by the lining.

Shoulder pads can be bought ready-made in different thicknesses, although the thinnest pads are usually suitable for most garments. Shoulder pads are easy to make yourself and you can adjust the thickness to suit your needs.

Making shoulder pads

Shoulder pads are usually made from a wool batting, which should be dry cleaned as it tends to become lumpy if it is washed. For dresses and blouses, thin polyester fiberfill should be used, since it is washable.

If the fabric of the garment is unsuitable for covering the pad, other fabrics, such as thin cottons, silk or synthetic crepe, can be used, if they complement the color of the main garment.

Occasionally pads are made from lightweight foam rubber and may need removing for cleaning or laundering. If this is the case, cover the pad on both sides and catch-stitch at shoulder and armhole seams.

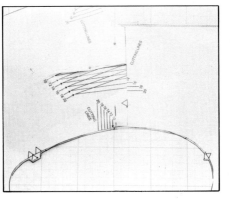

1 Pin in place any darts or seams which are included in the shoulder seam. Pin the front and back bodice pieces together at the shoulder seam only. Spread the pattern flat and mark the neck and armhole edges and seamlines as shown.

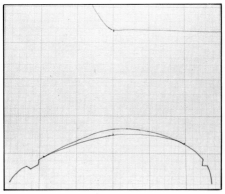

2 Draw in the sleeve edge of the pad. First measure 4in (10cm) down cutting lines on the back and front armhole edge. Using a flexible curve, join the two points, taking the line $\frac{1}{4}$in (6mm) into the seam allowance at the shoulder line.

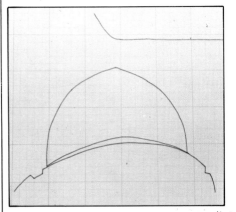

3 Draw the inner edge of the pad by measuring 1in (2.5cm) in from the neck seamline at the shoulder and joining this point to each end of the sleeve edge of the pad using a flexible curve. Cut out the pattern.

4 Cut out two shoulder pad pieces from the batting. Cut out a second pair of pads using the same pattern piece, then trim away $\frac{1}{4}$in (6mm) around the inner, deeply curved edge. If you need thick pads, cut a third pair (one for each pad) and trim away $\frac{3}{8}$in (1cm) from the inner edge.

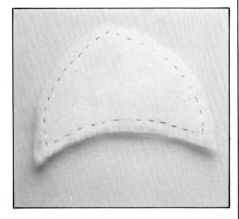

5 Place the pads together with the armhole edges aligned. Sew the layers together with a long running stitch all around the edge of the pad. Do not pull the thread tightly or the pad will pucker and pull out of shape.

Inserting the pads into a garment

Shoulder pads can be pinned into the garment while it is on a dressmaker's form, or you can pin them into the garment and then try it on.
The placement of the pad will be dictated by the style of the garment.
The pad edge can either be lined up with the armhole seam or moved outward to support the sleeve cap.

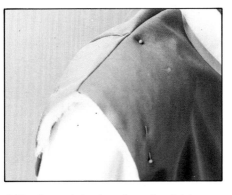

1 Pin the pads in place from the right side of the garment so that the pins can be easily removed if the pad needs adjusting. Check that the pads are equal on both shoulders and are correctly positioned. Adjust them if necessary. Take off the garment.

2 Turn the garment wrong side out. At the armhole edge, sew the pad to the seam allowance with running stitches. Sew the deeply curved edge of the pad to the shoulder seam allowances. If the pads are inserted into a garment with a neck facing, keep the facing free while you sew the pad in place; then catch stitch the facing in place over the end of the pad.

Making stiffened belts

Stiffened belts have a neater, crisper look than soft tie belts. They are made with a special treated backing, called "belting," which will not lose its stiffness when it is washed or dry cleaned.
Belting is available in different widths, the width of the backing being the finished width of the belt. You will need your waist measurement plus approximately 6in (15cm) allowance for an overlap when buying the belting. Choose a buckle $\frac{1}{8}$in (3mm) wider at the crossbar than the width of the belt backing.

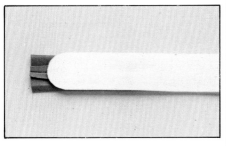

1 Cut a piece of fabric the length of the belting, plus $\frac{3}{4}$in (2cm), by twice the width of the belting, plus $\frac{3}{4}$in (2cm). Fold fabric with right sides together and stitch $\frac{3}{8}$in (1cm) from long raw edge. Center seam on back of belt and press open. Trim seam allowances to $\frac{1}{4}$in (6mm).

2 With sharp scissors, shape the end of the belting into a curve or point, depending on the effect you wish to achieve. Lay the belting over the belt fabric so that the point falls $\frac{3}{8}$in (1cm) from the end.

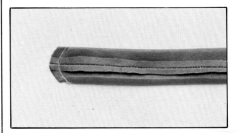

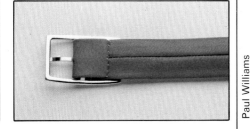

3 Draw around the shaped end with tailor's chalk. Stitch along the chalked line. Trim the seam allowances and clip the point. Turn the belt right side out and press flat, making sure that the seam lies on the center of the back.

4 Push the shaped end of the belting into the belt until it is in place. Turn in the ends of the belt fabric at the flat end and slip stitch them together.

5 If you are using a buckle with a prong, insert a metal eyelet or sew a buttonhole eyelet 1in (2.5cm) from the straight end of the belt. Slip the buckle onto the belt and the prong through the eyelet. Overcast the straight end firmly in place behind the buckle.

continued

Paul Williams

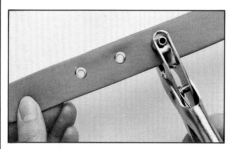

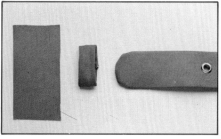

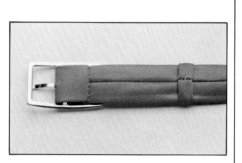

6 Try on the belt and mark the positions for the eyelets on the shaped end. Use metal or hand sewn eyelets to correspond to that used for the buckle prong.

7 To make a belt carrier, cut a strip of fabric 1⅛in (3cm) wide by twice the width of the belt plus ½in (1.2cm). Fold the fabric with the right sides together, and with the long raw edges matching, stitch ¼in (6mm) from the edge. Turn the tube right side out and press the seam to the center of the back of the tube.

8 Sew the short ends together with the right sides facing and overcast the raw edges. The seam should be ¼in (6mm) from the raw edge. Slip the carrier onto the belt and catch stitch it in place on the back of the belt if desired.

Sophisticated lady

Padded shoulders give this jacket its style. Directions for the straight skirt are given in the next course.

Adapting the pattern

Measurements
The pattern for this soft, unlined jacket is made by altering the pattern for the jacket in the Stitch by Stitch Pattern Pack, available in sizes 10-20, corresponding to sizes 8-18 in ready-made clothes.

Materials
Three sheets of tracing paper 31½in x 15¾in (80cm x 40cm)
Yardstick or ruler; flexible curve
Right triangle

1 Trace the jacket front and back, allowing enough paper to extend the center front out 2⅜in (6cm).

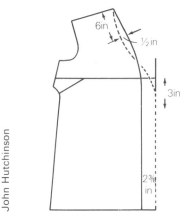

2 On the jacket front, measure out 2⅜in (6cm) from the center front line and draw the new front line.

Extend top line of dart to the new front edge. Measure down 3in (7.5cm) from the horizontal line and mark this point. Measure 6in (15cm) down the front edge from the shoulder; mark a point ½in (1.2 cm) in from the cutting line. With a flexible curve, join the two points just marked to the neck and front edges to form the new front curve. Seam allowances of ⅜in (1cm) have been included in these measurements.

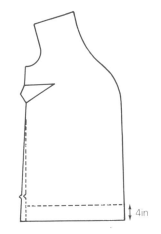

3 At the lower edge of the pattern, measure up 4in (10cm) all along to mark the new cutting line. The length can be adjusted but if you make the jacket longer than this adaptation, check to make sure the pattern pieces still fit into the quantities of fabric given for your size. A 1⅝in (4cm) hem allowance has been included in these measurements.

4 Measure across the pattern from the center front to the side edge just below the bust dart. Measure the same distance along the new lower edge and mark this point. Check that new measurements will fit your hips comfortably and adjust if necessary. Draw the new side edge from below the dart to the point just marked. Re-draw the notch on the side seam.

Lay jacket back tracing over front with the original side seam notches matching and trace the new side seamline and lower edge on the back pattern piece.

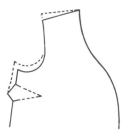

5 On the jacket front, square the shoulder by measuring up ⅜in (1cm) from the cutting line at the armhole edge. Join this point to the cutting line at the neck edge. The armhole now needs to be raised. Trace the original shoulder line and armhole curve. Lay the tracing over the pattern with the shoulder on the new shoulder line. Mark the armhole curve. Join the underarm point of the new curve to the dart point. Re-draw the shoulder and armhole curve in the same way on the jacket back.

John Hutchinson

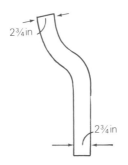

6 For front facing pattern, lay tracing paper over new jacket front pattern. Draw around front edge and along shoulder and hem edges. Measure 2¾in (7cm) along shoulder and hemline and draw a line parallel to front edge. Cut out.

7 Cut pattern for back facing as above.

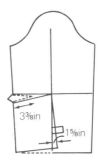

8 Trace the sleeve pattern leaving enough space to extend the lower edge down 12¼in (31cm). Extend the side seams down 12¼in (31cm) from the lower edge of the original sleeve. Extend the grain line to the lower edge. Measure from your underarm to elbow point and mark this distance on the left-hand (back) side seam of the sleeve. Draw a line at this point at a right angle to the grain line. Slash up the grain line and along the horizontal line until the slashes almost meet. At the lower sleeve edge, lap the left-hand side of the sleeve 1⅝in (4cm) over the right and tape in place. Tape paper under the horizontal slash which has now opened halfway up the sleeve. Mark a point in the center of the slash, 3⅜in (8.5cm) from the cutting line at the sleeve edge. Join the outer edges of the slash to the point to form the elbow dart and draw the cutting edge. Re-draw the lower sleeve edge as shown.

9 Cut sleeve facings 2¾in (7cm) deep, using sleeve pattern as guide.
10 Draw a rectangle 2¾in (7cm) wide by waist measurement plus 6in (15cm) for belt.

Tony Boase

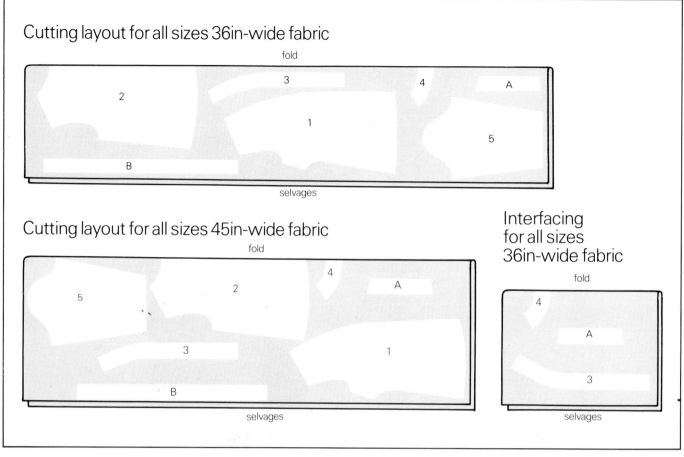

Cutting layout for all sizes 36in-wide fabric

fold

selvages

Cutting layout for all sizes 45in-wide fabric

fold

selvages

Interfacing for all sizes 36in-wide fabric

fold

selvages

John Hutchinson

Directions for making

Suggested fabrics
Linen, heavy cotton, lightweight wool, silk.

Materials
36in (90cm)-wide fabric with or
   without nap:
   Sizes 10, 12 and 14: 3yd (2.7m)
   Sizes 16, 18 and 20: 3⅜yd (3m)
45in (115cm)-wide fabric with or
   without nap:
   Sizes 10, 12 and 14: 2¼yd (2m)
   Sizes 16, 18 and 20: 2½yd (2.2m)
Matching thread
36in (90cm)-wide contrasting fabric
   for cording:
   For all sizes: ⅝yd (50cm)
1 card of bias binding
36in (90cm)-wide lightweight
   batting for shoulder pads:
   All sizes: 6in (15cm)
3⅜yd (3m) dressmaker's cord
1in (2.5cm)-wide belting to
   waist measurement plus 6in
   (15cm)
Belt buckle and eyelets

Key to adjusted pattern pieces
1 Jacket front   Cut 2
2 Jacket back   Cut 1 on fold
3 Front facing   Cut 2
4 Back neck facing Cut 1 on fold
5 Sleeve   Cut 2

A Sleeve facing   Cut 2
B Belt   Cut 1
For interfacing, use pieces 3, 4 and A

1 Adjust the pattern pieces and draw the pattern for the belt as shown on pages 62-63.
2 Prepare the fabric and pin on the pattern pieces as shown in the layout. Make sure that the straight grain line of the pattern lies on the straight grain of the fabric. Cut out the pieces, closely following outlines of pattern pieces. From the contrasting fabric cut bias strip 1¾in (4.5cm) wide to make a total length of 2⅞yd (2.6m).
3 Transfer all markings from the pattern to the fabric.
4 Staystitch the front and neck edges of the jacket to prevent them from stretching. With right sides together, join the bias strips to make the required length. Press the small seams open.

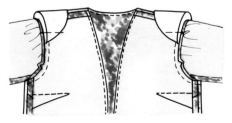

5 Pin and baste the bust and shoulder darts. Pin and baste the side and shoulder

seams. Pin and baste the elbow dart, then join the sleeve seams. Pin and baste the sleeve into the jacket and insert the shoulder pads, pinning them in place. Try on the jacket to make sure that it fits well. Make sure the elbow dart falls on the point of the elbow. Mark any necessary alterations.

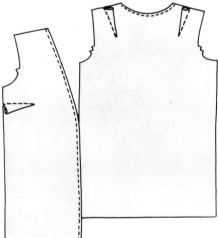

6 Remove the shoulder pads, rip out the armhole, sleeve, side and shoulder seams. Stitch the bust and shoulder darts. Press the bust darts down and the shoulder darts toward the center back.
7 Pin, baste and stitch the shoulder and side seams with the right sides together,

making any necessary alterations. Press seams open and finish seam allowances.

8 Baste interfacing to facing. With right sides together, join front and back neck facings at the shoulder seams. Press seams open. Trim interfacing close to stitching lines. Trim $\frac{1}{4}$in (6mm) from outer unseamed edge of interfacing close to stitching lines. Finish edge of facing by turning under and stitching.
9 Cover the cord with the bias strip to make cording (see Volume 8, page 53). Cut a piece of cording to go around front neck edge of jacket.

10 Place cording and facing along jacket front edge, right sides facing and edges matching. Pin, baste and stitch. Grade seam allowances and understitch

through seam allowance of jacket and interfaced facing, incorporating the seam allowance on cording. Press.
11 Sew two rows of gathering stitches around the sleeve cap between the notches. Fold, baste and stitch the elbow dart in each sleeve. Press the darts down. Baste and stitch the sleeve seams with right sides together. Press the seams open and finish seam allowances. Make cording and attach facing, interfacing and piping at the cuff as described for the neck and front facing.

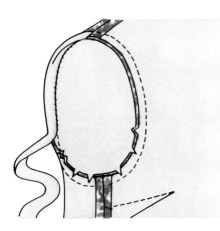

12 Pin, baste and stitch the sleeves into the armholes with the sleeve uppermost on the machine. Press seam allowances toward the sleeve and clip the curved edges. Trim seam allowances and finish them with bias binding.

13 From the batting, make shoulder pads as described on page 60.

From scraps of fabric cut two pieces 1in (2.5cm) larger all around than the shoulder pads. Place each pad on the fabric, turn in the edges, and catch stitch in place all around to cover one side of the pad. Insert the pads into the jacket as shown on page 60.

14 Try on the jacket and check the length. Mark the hem. Turn up the hem allowance and finish the raw edge with overcasting or by turning under $\frac{1}{4}$in (6mm) and stitching close to the fold. Sew the hem in place. Turn under raw edge at lower edge of facing and slip stitch to hem. Press the folded hem edge only.
15 Make a stiffened belt as shown on page 61. At waist level on the jacket side seams, make two thread belt carriers to hold the belt in place.

Terry Evans

Tony Boase

Sewing / COURSE 41

*Kick pleats
*Invisible zippers
*Straight skirt:
  adapting the pattern;
  directions for making

Kick pleats

Kick pleats are single pleats folded to the wrong side of a garment so that only a fold shows in the seam of the garment. They are often used on straight skirts or dresses to allow ease of movement.

The pleat can be pressed either to the left or the right, and the direction in which a pleat should be pressed is usually indicated on a commercial pattern. Careful pressing is essential; the pleat should have a sharp crease to give it a crisp look.

A kick pleat can either be incorporated into a seam or formed by a fold in the fabric. In these step-by-step directions we show a seamed pleat, but the procedure is essentially the same for both types of pleat.

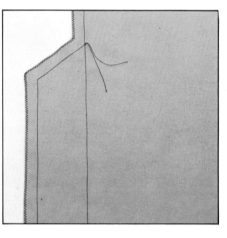

1 Transfer all markings from the pattern to the fabric. Baste and stitch the shaped seam from the hem edge to the waist. Machine baste from the release point of the pleat—the edge of the straight seam—to the hem edge. Clip into the seam allowance at the release point. Finish seam allowances, press them together and press the pleat to one side.

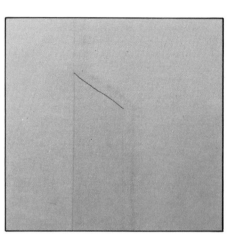

2 From the right side press the pleat again.
To hold the pleat in place, topstitch from the release point to the pleat edge. Remove the machine basting.

Invisible zippers

Invisible zippers, as the name suggests, hardly show when they are inserted into a garment. The zipper opening looks like a plain seam with only the zipper tab showing at the top of the opening.

This type of zipper is inserted into the garment in a completely different way from an ordinary zipper. It is stitched to the seam allowances only and no stitching is visible from the right side.

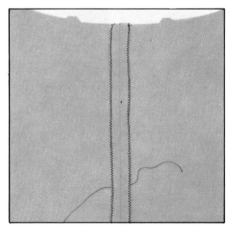

1 Machine baste the zipper opening on the seamline. Press the seam open carefully and finish the edges. Press again.

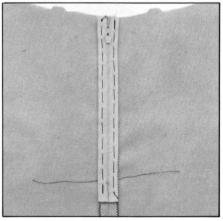

2 Place the zipper, face down, over the seam allowances on the wrong side of the garment. The teeth should be centered over the seam. Baste each side of the zipper tape to allowances only; do not catch right side of fabric in basting.

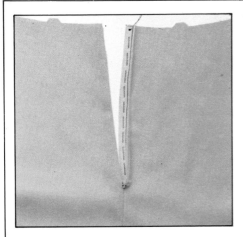

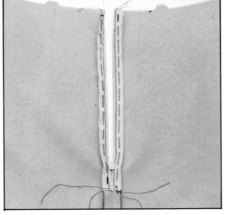

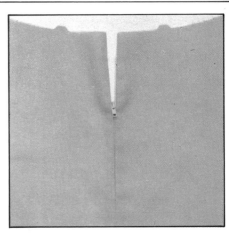

3 Rip out the basting and open the zipper to the base. Spread the left hand tape flat and stitch down the zipper close to the zipper teeth. The stitches should go through the seam allowance only.

4 Repeat with the opposite side of the zipper.

5 Finish the thread ends securely by backstitching down to the end of the tape. Press zipper lightly, wrong side down on a pad.

Slim-line skirt

Adapting the pattern

Measurements
The pattern for this straight skirt is made by adapting the pattern for the A-line skirt from the Stitch by Stitch Pattern Pack, available in sizes 10-20; corresponding to sizes 8-18 in ready-made clothes.

Materials
2 sheets of tracing paper, at least $31\frac{1}{2}$x$19\frac{1}{2}$in (80x50cm)
Yardstick or ruler

This smart lined skirt is a perfect partner for the unlined jacket in the previous course, on page 64.

On the skirt front, measure in 4in (10cm) from the side edge at the hem edge and mark this point. Measure down 6in (15cm) from the waist edge on the cutting line. Using a long ruler, join the two points. A $\frac{5}{8}$in (1.5cm) seam allowance has been included.
Repeat for the side edge of the back of the skirt, again starting 6in (15cm) from the waist and reducing the width by 4in (10cm).

on center back line and mark a point for the top of the pleat. Draw a line $2\frac{3}{8}$in (6cm) outside, and parallel to, the center back line. Mark the top of this line $16\frac{1}{2}$in (42cm) from the waist edge of the skirt. Join the two points just marked to form a slanting line for the top of the pleat. Draw in a $\frac{5}{8}$in (1.5cm) seam allowance down the whole of the back edge.

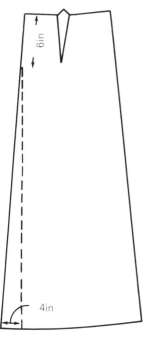

1 Trace the skirt back and front pattern pieces.

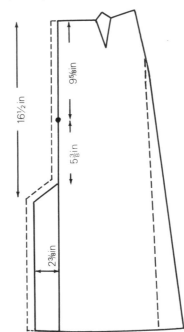

2 On the skirt back, mark the dot for the base of zipper, $9\frac{5}{8}$in (24.5cm) below waist on the center back line. Measure down 15in (38cm) from the waist edge

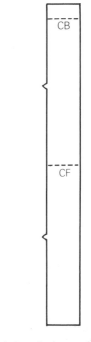

3 On waistband, change "left side" to "center back" and mark center front halfway between "CB" and stitching line at the other end. Measure original front section of waistband; mark this distance on pattern with notches (at side seams).

Paul Williams

John Hutchinson

Directions for making

Cutting layout for 36in/45in-wide fabric — with or without nap

Cutting layout for 36in-wide lining fabric

Cutting layout for 36in-wide interfacing

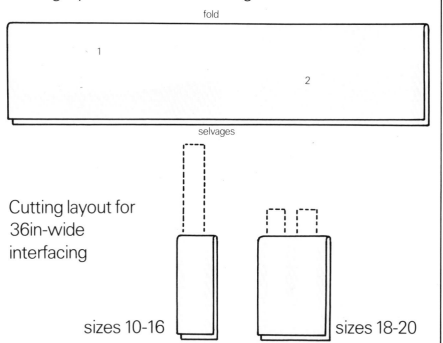

sizes 10-16

sizes 18-20

John Hutchinson

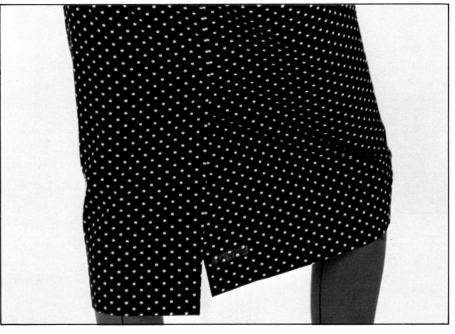

Suggested fabrics
Medium-weight fabrics with body such as gabardine, hopsacking, worsted, linen.

Materials
36in (90cm)-wide or 45in (115cm)-fabric with or without nap:
Sizes 10, 12 and 14: $2\frac{1}{8}$yd (1.9m)
Sizes 16, 18 and 20: $2\frac{1}{4}$yd (2m)
36in (90cm)-wide lining fabric:
Sizes 10, 12 and 14: $2\frac{1}{8}$yd (1.9m)
Sizes 16, 18 and 20: $2\frac{1}{4}$yd (2m)
36in (90cm)-wide interfacing:
Sizes 10-16: 6in (15cm)
Sizes 18 and 20: 10in (25cm)
9in (23cm) invisible skirt zipper
Matching thread; hook and eye
Waist length of grosgrain ribbon

Key to adjusted pattern pieces
1 Skirt front   Cut 1 on fold
2 Skirt back   Cut 2
3 Waistband   Cut 1
Interfacing: use piece 3

1 Alter the three pattern pieces for the skirt as shown on page 67.
2 Prepare the fabric and pin on the pattern pieces following the layout given. Make sure that the grain line of the pattern lies on the straight grain of the fabric.
Cut out the pieces, carefully following the edge of the newly cut pattern.
3 Transfer all markings from the pattern to the fabric and remove the pattern pieces.
4 Prepare the lining fabric and pin on the skirt front pattern piece. On the skirt back pattern, fold the pleat section to the wrong side in line with the upper part of the center back edge so that the pleat is eliminated. Pin pattern piece in place and cut out front and back pieces, following the cutting lines.
Cut out the waistband from interfacing, to the foldline only.
5 Transfer all markings from the pattern pieces to the lining using tailor's tacks or dressmaker's chalk. Remove the pattern pieces.

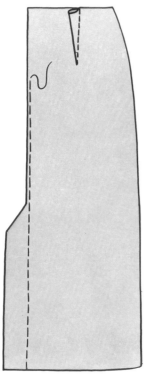

6 Baste the front and back waist darts. With right sides together, baste the skirt backs together down the center back line from the hem, up the pleat foldline and the back seamline to the base of the zipper opening. This eliminates the pleat. Baste the skirt front and back together at the side seams. Baste the skirt to a temporary waistband made from a piece of grosgrain ribbon.
Try on the skirt and make any necessary fitting alterations (see Volume 3, pages 62–63).
Mark the alterations with basting or tailor's chalk.

Remove the waistband and rip out the basting in the side seams.

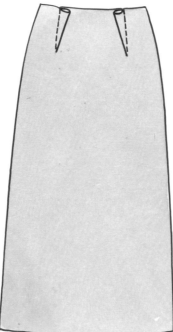

7 Stitch the front and back darts and press them toward the center of the skirt.

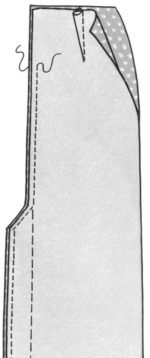

8 Machine baste along the pleat foldline from the hem to the top of the pleat. Baste the remainder of the center back seam around the pleat and stitch the seam from the hemline to the base of the zipper. Finish the seam allowances and make the kick pleat as shown on page 66.
Finish raw edges of center back seam and press open.

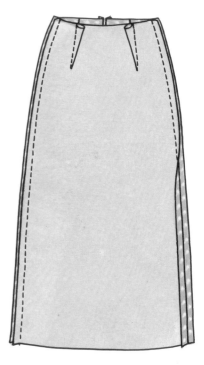

9 Baste and stitch the side seams. Press the seams open and finish the raw edges.
10 Insert invisible zipper into center back opening as shown on page 66.

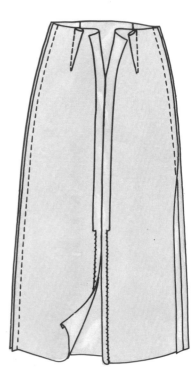

11 Baste and stitch the waist darts in the lining back and front. Press them to the center. Stitch the center back seam from the top of the pleat to the base of the zipper. Press seams open. Turn under and sew narrow hems on the center back edges below the seam. Finish remaining seam allowances. With right sides together, baste and stitch side seams. Press seams open and finish seam allowances.

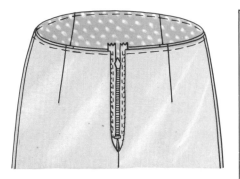

12 Slip the lining over the skirt with wrong sides together. Baste the skirt and lining together around the waist edge and slip stitch the lining to the zipper tape.
13 If necessary, piece the interfacing for the waistband. Baste and catch-stitch the interfacing to the wrong side of the notched edge of the waistband.
14 Baste and stitch the interfaced edge of the waistband to the skirt. Grade the seam allowances, trimming interfacing close to the stitching. Press the seam toward the waistband.

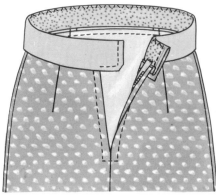

15 Fold the waistband on the foldline with right sides together and stitch across the short ends. Clip the corners and trim the interfacing close to the stitching.
16 Turn the waistband right side out. Turn under the raw edge on the inside of the waistband and hand-hem it to the stitching. Press. Attach a hook and eye to the waistband above the zipper.

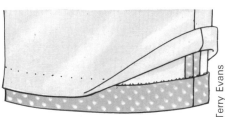

Terry Evans

17 Try on the skirt and mark the hem. Turn up the skirt hem only and hand-hem in place.
Trim $\frac{3}{8}$in (1cm) from the lining hem and turn up the same hem allowance as on skirt. Hem and press. This makes the lining $\frac{3}{8}$in (1cm) shorter than the skirt.

Getting it together

Accessories can turn this simple skirt into something special for any occasion—try it with a scarf, a shapely belt or a simple rope.

Ray Duns

Shoestring

Floating fish

Babies and children love mobiles! And this one, made of playful patchwork fish, will brighten up any nursery or bedroom.

Finished size
Each fish is 4¼ × 3½in (11 × 9cm).

Materials

Scraps of cotton fabric: two different but harmonizing prints and one solid color for each fish
4in (10cm) square of felt in a harmonizing color for each fish
Scraps of black and white felt
Matching sewing thread
Transparent nylon thread
Polyester stuffing
Two 12in (30.5cm) pieces of florists' wire
Four small jump rings
Fabric glue
Tracing paper
Thin cardboard
Iron-on interfacing
Pinking shears

1 Fold the tracing paper and trace each of the three shapes on it, placing the fold on the broken line to obtain the complete shapes. Cut them out.
2 Trace around the shapes on cardboard and cut out three cardboard templates.
3 Place each cardboard template on the matte side of the interfacing and draw around it. Draw two heads (pink shape), two diamond body shapes and four triangle body shapes. Cut them out.
4 Place interfacing pieces, shiny side down, on the different harmonizing fabrics, using the solid color for the head. Leave a margin of at least ⅜in (1cm) around each piece. Iron the interfacing in place. Cut out each piece, adding ⅜in (1cm) seam allowance.
5 Carefully fold the seam allowances to the wrong side; pin and baste them in place.
6 Assemble the fish, one side at a time, by placing adjoining patches together, right sides facing and edges matching, and working along the edges with tiny overcasting stitches. Begin by joining the triangular body pieces to the diamond body piece. Then sew the head to the body. Repeat to make the other side of the fish.
7 Using the templates for the head and the triangular body piece and a harmonizing shade of felt, cut one large and two small felt triangles for tail and fins. Use pinking shears for the back edges (see photo).
8 Place the two sides of the fish together with right sides facing. Place the two fins

Brian Nash

between them, pointing inward, with front edges about ⅜in (1cm) from head seam. Baste around edges, catching in fins, then overcast around outer edges, leaving 1¼in (3cm) unstitched on each side of tail point. Remove all basting threads. Turn the fish right side out.
9 Place tail in opening and pin it in place on one side. Stuff the fish loosely. Pin the opening edges together and slip stitch them, catching in all layers.
10 From white felt cut out two ¾in (2cm)-diameter circles for outer eyes, using pinking shears. Cut two ⅜in (1cm) circles from black felt for inner eyes.
11 Glue a black circle to the center of each white one, then glue the eyes in place on each side of the head.

12 Sew a jump ring to the top of the head.
13 Repeat steps 3 to 12 to make three more fish.
14 Twist one piece of wire in the center to form a loop. Bend each end to form hooks. Prepare another wire in the same way.
15 Cut four 6in (15cm) pieces of nylon thread. Tie one end of each to the jump ring on a fish and tie the other to one end of a wire.
16 Suspend one wire from the other with an 11in (28cm) piece of thread.
17 Make a 6in (15cm) long loop and tie it to the central loop in the top wire.
18 Hang up the mobile. Adjust the threads if necessary so that the fish hang evenly.

*Stretch fabric binding
*Casing for waist elastic
*T-shirt dress:
  adapting the pattern;
  directions for making

Stretch fabric binding

Binding used to finish and strengthen a raw edge can also be used to add a decorative trim to a garment. On the T-shirt dress, overleaf, which is made in a stretch fabric, the binding replaces the neck and armhole facings. It can be made in a contrasting color, as shown in the step-by-step directions. When you are using a stretch fabric for binding strips, it is not necessary to cut the binding strips on the bias, as with woven fabrics (see Volume 1, page 56), because stretch fabrics already have the necessary "give" in them.

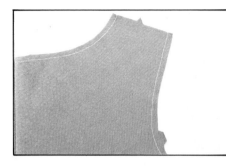

1 Staystitch around the edges to be bound (in this case the neck and armhole edges) to prevent unnecessary stretching and distortion of the fabric.

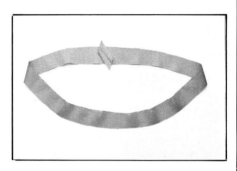

2 Measure the entire neck edge and armhole edges. Cut a strip of stretch fabric 1in (2.5cm) wide by the required length, plus ¼in (6mm) seam allowances at each end. Join each strip at the ends.

3 With the short seam at the center back of the neck, pin, baste and stitch binding to the neck edge, right sides together, taking a ¼in (6mm) seam allowance. On the right side, press the binding and seam allowances up, away from the garment.

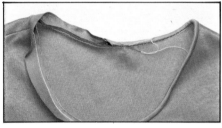

4 Turn in a ¼in (6mm) seam allowance on the unstitched edge of the binding and press. Fold the binding over the raw edge of the neckline to the inside and hem the folded edge to the stitching line. Press.

5 Apply the binding to the armhole edges in the same way, positioning the seam at the underarm seam.

Casing for waist elastic

The casing for the waist elastic on the dress on the next page is attached to the inside of the dress to form a channel for the elastic. It is made from the same fabric as the dress and does not need to be cut on the bias, since the stretch fabric has plenty of "give".

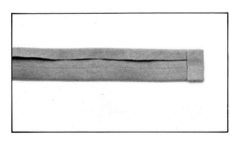

1 Turn in a ⅜in (1cm) seam allowance along both long edges of the casing and press flat, then turn in ⅝in (1.5cm) at each end. Press.

2 Transfer the casing position lines from the pattern to the garment with basting lines. Starting at one side seam, pin the casing to the inside of the dress between the two lines of basting around the entire waist.

continued

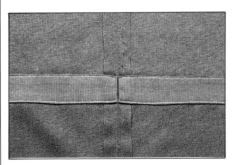

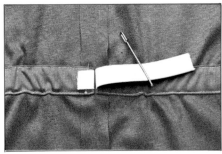

3 Baste the casing in place close to the edges. Using a very small zig-zag stitch, or stretching the fabric slightly if you are using a straight stitch, sew the casing in place, stitching close to the edges. Leave the ends open for inserting the elastic. Remove basting and press.

4 Cut a length of $\frac{3}{4}$in (2cm)-wide elastic to fit around the waist, plus a $\frac{3}{4}$in (2cm) seam allowance for joining. Anchor one end of the elastic at the opening with a pin and thread the other end through the casing using a tapestry needle or safety pin. Distribute the fullness evenly around the waist and check for fit.

5 Join the ends of the elastic together securely. Push the ends into the casing and slip stitch opening as shown in the top photograph. On the right side (bottom photograph), only the seamlines show.

Multi-purpose T-shirt dress

This simple, versatile T-shirt dress is quick to make and easy to wear. Choose your accessories with care and it will see you through the day and into the night. Wear it as a jumper over a shirt or sweater, or brighten it up with a cummerbund and slacks. On hot summer days wear it by itself or with a simple linen jacket; dress it up with a glittery stole for the evening.

Measurements

The dress is made by adapting the pattern for the T-shirt top from the Stitch by Stitch Pattern Pack, which is available in sizes 10-20, corresponding to sizes 8-18 in readymade clothes. The pattern alterations include $\frac{5}{8}$in (1.5cm) seam allowances, except at the neck and armhole edges, which are bound and do not need a seam allowance.

Adapting the pattern

Materials

Two sheets of tracing paper at least 60×15in (150×40cm approx)
Flexible curve
Ruler or yardstick

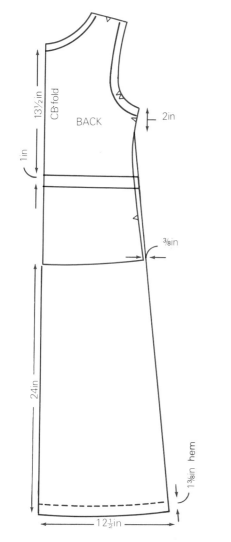

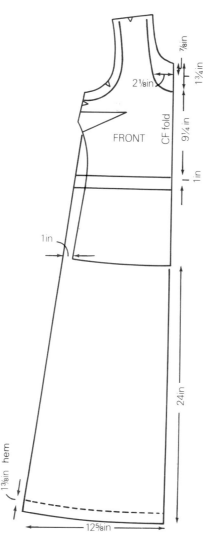

John Hutchinson

1 Trace the T-shirt back pattern onto the tracing paper, leaving enough room to extend the lower edge to dress length. Measure down 24in (61cm) at intervals around the hem and mark the lower edge of the dress. Measure out 12½in (32cm) from the center front line around the hem edge and mark the point.
2 Measure down the side cutting line and mark a point 2in (5cm) from the armhole cutting line. Mark a point ⅜in (1cm) out from the hem edge of the T-shirt pattern. Draw the new side cutting line through these two points and extend it at the same angle 24in (61cm) below the hem edge of the T-shirt for the side hem edge. Draw the hemline following the curve of the T-shirt hemline. A 1⅜in (3.5cm) hem allowance is included.
3 No seam allowance is needed at the neck and armhole edges, so trim away the seam allowances.
4 For the waistline casing position, measure 13½in (34.5cm) down the center back from the neck edge. Mark this point and then mark another point 1in (2.5cm) below it. Draw two horizontal lines across to the side cutting line.

The casing is positioned between these two lines.
5 For the front of the dress, trace the T-shirt front pattern and extend the center front line for 24in (61cm) from the hem edge of the T-shirt. Mark the lower edge of the dress and measure out to the side edge as described for the back. Mark a point 1in (2.5cm) out from the hemline of the T-shirt top. Draw the new side cutting line from the bottom line of the bust dart, through the marked point to the hem at the lower edge of the dress.
6 For the neckline, measure 1¾in (4.5cm) down the center front line from the neck edge. Draw a line at right angles to the front neckline, positioning it ⅞in (2.2cm) down from the original neck edge. Extend the line in for 2⅛in (5.5cm). Draw the new neck edge, from the neck seamline, curving it around through the marked points as shown.
No seam allowance is needed.
Trim away remaining seam allowance around neck and armhole edges.
7 To mark the waistline casing position, measure 9¼in (23.5cm) down from the new neck edge and mark. Measure down a further 1in (2.5cm) and mark. Draw

two horizontal lines across to the side cutting line as for the back.
8 For the casing, measure across the adapted front and back pattern pieces from the center front and center back to the new side seams.
Add the two measurements together and double this figure, then add ⅝in (1.5cm) seam allowance to each end. The casing is this length, and 1¾in (4.5cm) wide. The seam allowance down the side edges is ⅜in (1cm).

Directions for making

Materials
36in (90cm)-wide stretch fabric:
   Sizes 10, 12, 14, 16: 3⅛yd (2.8m)
   Sizes 18, 20: 3⅜yd (3m)
60in (150cm)-wide stretch fabric:
   Sizes 10, 12, 14, 16: 1⅝yd (1.4m)
   Sizes 18, 20: 1¾yd (1.5m)
Contrasting fabric for binding:
   All sizes and widths: 4in (10cm)
Matching synthetic thread
¾in (2cm)-wide elastic; waist
   measurement plus ¾in (2cm)

Note If you have adjusted the length of the dress, alter the fabric quantities accordingly. Check the cutting layout, using the pattern adaptations already cut, before buying any fabric.

1 Prepare the fabric and cut out the pattern pieces. Transfer all the pattern markings using dressmaker's carbon, tailor's chalk or lines of basting, before the fabric stretches out of shape.

Cutting layout for
60in-wide
stretch fabric
without nap

fold

1

BINDING

selvages

Key to adapted pattern pieces
1 Dress front   Cut 1
                 on fold
2 Dress back   Cut 1
                 on fold
A Casing   Cut 1
                 on fold

fold

2

A

open fabric to cut

Cutting layout for
36in-wide
stretch fabric
with or without nap

fold

Cutting layout for 60in-wide stretch
fabric for contrasting color binding

1

2

CASING
BINDING

selvages

John Hutchinson

Victor Yuan

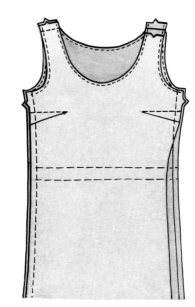

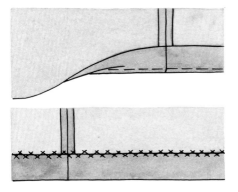

3 Baste the shoulder and side seams. Make any necessary alterations to the fit. Stitch shoulder and side seams, right sides together, matching casing markings. Press seams open.

5 Try on the dress and mark the hem. Turn up the hem and baste close to folded line. Hem with herringbone stitch, as shown in Volume 4, page 61. Remove basting and press the folded edge only.

2 Staystitch neck and armhole edgings, following directions in Volume 4, page 63. Pin, baste and stitch bust darts, with right sides together. Press down.

4 Cut binding and apply to the neck and armhole edges, as shown on page 73. Make the casing on the inside of the dress and insert the elastic, following the directions on pages 73-74.

Terry Evans

Needlework/ *COURSE 12*

Pulled thread work

Pulled thread work is a type of counted-thread embroidery in which the stitches are drawn together with varying degrees of tension, thus pulling apart the threads of the fabric to create a lacy, open effect. It differs from drawn thread work mainly in that no threads are removed from the fabric. Stitches may also be worked normally, without pulling, to create a textural contrast with those which are pulled and with the openings formed by them.

Materials

The fabrics suitable for this work are those with an even weave—that is, the same number of warp and weft threads per inch (or centimeter), woven in a plain over-and-under pattern. The fabric should also be fairly loosely woven, so that the threads will move easily, although very flimsy fabrics may present problems in laundering, as the threads around the stitched areas may become displaced.

The range of suitable weights is quite wide—from fine handkerchief linen and organdy to coarse fabrics such as hopsacking and burlap. Some sheer synthetic curtain fabrics are well suited to pulled thread work. The fabric you choose will depend, naturally, on the type of article you are making.

For the sachet cover and stocking bag, right, we have used fine even-weave cotton; for place mats a medium-weight linen would be most appropriate; for a panel or hanging you could use any weight of fabric. Test the fabric's suitability by making a sample first.

White is the traditional color used for pulled thread work, but you can, of course, use any other color you like.

Normally the thread used is in a color matching or harmonizing with the fabric. The attractive quality of pulled thread results from the interaction of fabric and stitches, rather than from the stitches themselves, and a strongly contrasting thread tends to emphasize the stitches at the expense of the texture and pattern.

In general, the thread should be of the same thickness as that used in the fabric, and it should have a firm quality. *Coton à broder*, pearl cotton, buttonhole twist, and crochet cotton are good choices, depending on the fabric. Stranded embroidery floss can be used on fine fabrics—as for the project right, but it tends to fray when used on heavier fabrics.

Always use a tapestry needle, which slips between the threads without splitting them. A relatively large needle will help to separate the threads a little before you pull up the stitch.

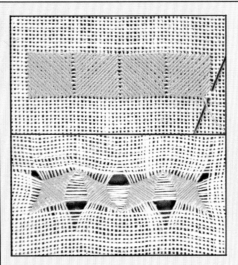

Satin stitch blocks

This is a frequently-used stitch, essentially the same as flat stitch in needlepoint (see Volume 8, page 86). When the thread is pulled, as in the lower example, a diamond shape is produced. In these samples the stitch is worked over 12 threads, as in the sachet case.

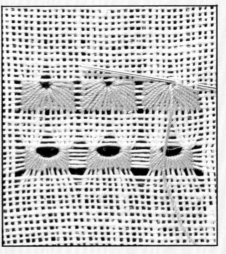

Half eyelets

Eyelet stitch, as the name suggests, makes a hole in the fabric. The stitch is often worked in a square shape; in this variation, used for the sachet case, it forms half a square. The upper example shows the stitches worked without pulling the thread. In the lower example the thread has been pulled tightly to produce a larger hole. In both rows the stitches are worked over 10 vertical and 5 horizontal threads, as in the sachet case.

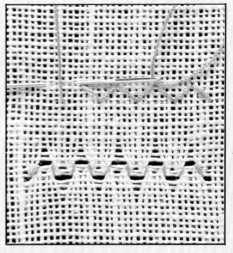

Zig-zag backstitch

This is simply backstitch worked in a zig-zag pattern. In this sample each stitch crosses 3 vertical and 3 horizontal threads. When the stitches are pulled tightly, as in the lower row, an open effect is produced.

Fred Mancini

Using a frame

The use of a frame is recommended, as it makes it easier to count the threads and to maintain an even tension.

As in other kinds of embroidery, it is important that the fabric be taut in the frame. If you are using a hoop type of frame, adjust the size of the outer ring before inserting the fabric. Lay the fabric smoothly over the inner ring, then press the outer ring over it. The fabric should be perfectly smooth and taut; if it isn't, remove the outer ring, tighten the screw a little and try again.

If the fabric is delicate lay a few sheets of tissue paper over the fabric before positioning the outer ring. Once the outer ring is in place, tear away the tissue from the working area.

Instead of a hoop you may prefer to use an artist's stretcher frame, which can be bought in an art supply store and is easily assembled. Attach the fabric to the frame with thumbtacks or staples, being careful to keep it straight. Both frame and fabric should be large enough so that the edges can be trimmed away when the work is finished.

In using any kind of frame you must work with an up-and-down stabbing motion. This can be done with one hand, but if you have a standing frame you can use both hands. If you are right-handed, keep your right hand under the work and give your left hand the easier task of working on top.

Beginning and ending work

For some pulled thread designs, particularly symmetrical ones, you should begin by marking the center of the fabric with two lines of basting. These help in positioning the motifs. To begin stitching, either darn the thread into the fabric along the line to be covered with stitching (beginning with a backstitch to secure it), or knot the end and proceed as shown in Needlework course 1, Volume 1, page 69. To finish a thread, darn it into the underside of the work. Do not take the thread from one stitched area to another; it will show through on the right side.

Peter Pugh-Cook/Designed by Moyra McNeill

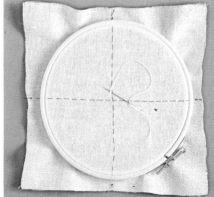

Fred Mancini

Perfect match

Add a bit of luxury — and a sweet fragrance — to your lingerie drawer with this matching sachet and stocking/pantyhose bag embroidered in pulled thread work.

Finished size
Bag, when closed, measures $8 \times 6\frac{1}{2}$in (20.5×16.5cm).
Sachet, empty, measures $3\frac{3}{8}$in (8.5cm) square.

Materials (for both items)
$\frac{1}{2}$yd (.4m) of even-weave fabric, any width (fabric A), having about 32 threads to 1in (2.5cm) (see Note)
$\frac{1}{2}$yd (.4m) of lining fabric, any width (fabric B)
Piece of medium-weight interfacing, 14 x 9in (35.5 x 23cm)
1 skein of stranded embroidery floss in a matching or harmonizing color
Tapestry needle, size 24-26
6in (15cm) diameter embroidery hoop
$1\frac{1}{8}$yd (1m) of ribbon, $\frac{3}{4}$in (2cm) wide
Pot pourri

Note The amounts and measurements given in these instructions are based on fabric with approximately 32 threads to 1in (2.5cm). If fabric with more or fewer threads is used, you will need to adapt the chart in order to keep the work the same size. For example, the square blocks of satin stitch are shown worked across 12 vertical and 12 horizontal threads. If your fabric has 20 threads to 1in (2.5cm) you should work the blocks over 8 threads (two-thirds of 12) to keep the stitches roughly the same size.

To make the sachet

1 Cut a piece of fabric A 8×11in (20.5× 28cm). Measure 8in (20.5cm) from one end and baste across the fabric at this point. Divide this square into quarters with two more lines of basting.
2 Place the fabric in the frame, with the intersection of basting in the center.
3 Work the center design following the chart, overleaf, and starting with the stitch marked. (See stitch samples, left.) We used one strand of embroidery floss, but if your fabric is heavier you will need to use more strands, or a thicker type of thread. Use a length about 24in (60cm) long. In order to achieve a lacy effect you must pull the stitches very tightly.

4 When you have finished embroidering the center motif, add the edging stitch (see left), positioning it 12 threads outside the outer half-eyelets.
5 Remove the completed embroidery from the frame; remove the basting and press the work on the wrong side.
6 Fold the fabric widthwise, $\frac{1}{4}$in (6mm) outside the edge stitching, wrong sides together, and finger-press this fold. Pin the two layers together around the edges, then carefully trim away the excess fabric, leaving a margin of $\frac{3}{4}$in (2cm) outside the edge stitching. Open the fabric flat.

7 Cut two pieces of fabric B the same size as the opened out embroidered fabric.
8 Place one of the lining pieces right side up on a flat surface and lay the embroidered piece on top of it, also right side up. Lay the remaining piece of lining on top, right side down. Baste and stitch around the edges, taking $\frac{1}{2}$in (1.2cm) seams and leaving a gap of 2in (5cm) along one long side. Grade the seam and turn the case right side out.
9 Push the stitching to the edge, taking special care at the corners. Tuck in the seam allowances along the gap. Press all around and slip stitch the opening edges.
10 Fold the case in half, with the embroidered layer outside, forming a square. Overcast the edges together.
11 Fill with pot pourri; overcast top edges.

To make the stocking bag

1 Cut a piece of fabric A measuring 14×9in (36×23cm). Fold it in half widthwise and baste along the fold line to divide into two equal areas.
2 Divide one of these areas into quarters with lines of basting, as for sachet.
3 Place the fabric in the frame with the intersection of basting in the middle.
4 Starting at the center point, measure out $1\frac{7}{8}$in (4.7cm) along the horizontal line of basting. This is the center point of the right-hand motif. Work the motif, following the chart, then work the left-hand motif in the same way.
5 Work two lines of zig-zag back stitch parallel to the center basting, positioning them 9 threads in from the square blocks closest to the center. Move the fabric along in the frame to continue the edge stitching to the ends of the fabric. Remove basting and press the work.
6 Cut two pieces of fabric B the same size as the embroidered piece, for lining. Cut three more pieces: two pockets 12 x 8½in (30.5 x 21.5cm) and one envelope piece 6 x 9in (15 x 23cm).
7 Place one of the lining pieces on the embroidered piece, wrong sides facing; baste together $\frac{3}{8}$in (1cm) from the edges.
8 Turn under $\frac{1}{4}$in (6mm) and then $\frac{3}{8}$in (1cm) along one long edge of the envelope piece. Baste and hem by hand.
9 Lay the envelope piece on the second lining piece at one end, wrong side of envelope to right side of lining. Baste them together around the outer edges.
10 Place the lining/envelope right sides up on a flat surface and lay the embroidered cover, right side down, on top. motifs *away* from envelope.
11 Lay the piece of interfacing on top. Pin the layers together around all four sides, baste and stitch $\frac{1}{2}$in (1.2cm) from the edges, leaving a gap about 4in (10cm) wide at the short end away from the envelope. Grade the seam allowances.
12 Turn bag right side out. Push the stitching to the edge. Tuck in seam allowances

at the opening. Press all around. Close the opening with slip stitching.
13 Turn under $\frac{1}{4}$in (6mm) and then $\frac{3}{8}$in (1cm) along both short edges of each pocket piece. Baste in place and hand-hem.
14 Fold each pocket piece in half, wrong sides facing, and join sides with French seams. Turn pockets right side out; press.
15 Mark center points of pockets and envelope piece. Join pockets and envelope with tiny overcasting stitches, about 2in (5cm) to each side of center.
16 Baste and hand-sew the ribbon to the cover between the lines of edge stitching.

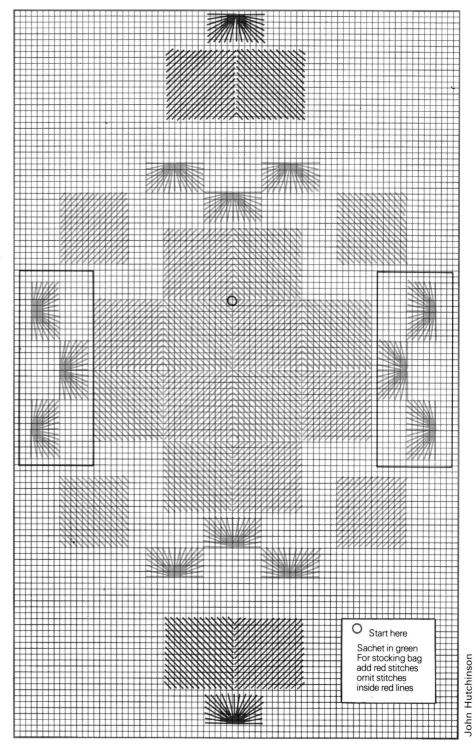

○ Start here

Sachet in green
For stocking bag
add red stitches
omit stitches
inside red lines

John Hutchinson

Peter Pugh-Cook

Shoestring

Make-up collection

A pretty and practical bag to keep your make-up neat in your handbag. It also has a pocket for your mirror.

Finished size
6¾×5in (17×13cm).

Materials
- ¼yd (.2m) of 36in (90cm)-wide printed cotton fabric
- ¼yd (.2m) of 36in (90cm)-wide nylon ciré for lining
- ¼yd (.2m) of 36in (90cm)-wide heavyweight interfacing
- 9in (23cm) zipper
- Matching sewing thread

1 From printed cotton fabric cut out two pieces, each 8×6¼in (20×16cm).
2 To form bag shape, fold one piece in half widthwise with right sides together. With fold on left-hand side, mark a point 3½in (9cm) down from right-hand edge. Draw a gradual curve from top fold to this point. Cut along curved line.
3 Repeat step 2 on other fabric piece.
4 Using one fabric piece as a pattern, cut two lining pieces and two interfacing pieces the same size.
5 For the mirror pocket, from printed cotton fabric cut one piece 5×3½in (13×9cm). Cut one lining and one interfacing piece the same size.
6 Place printed pocket and pocket lining together with right sides facing. Place interfacing pocket on wrong side of printed pocket. Pin, baste and stitch around edges taking ⅜in (1cm) seam allowance, leaving one long side open.
7 Trim corners and seam allowances. Turn pocket right side out. Turn in opening edges; slip stitch them together to close.
8 Pin and baste interfacing bag pieces to wrong side of printed bag pieces.
9 Place pocket on right side of one interfaced bag piece, centering it and placing lower edge 1¼in (3cm) up from bag's lower edge. Pin, baste and topstitch pocket in place.
10 Place bag pieces together with right sides facing. Pin, baste and stitch together at sides from marked points to lower edge, taking ¾in (2cm) seam allowance.
11 Turn under ¾in (2cm) on both top curved edges; pin and baste. Pin and baste zipper into top opening. Open zipper and topstitch it in place.
12 Pin, baste and stitch lower edges of bag together. Trim corners and seam allowance. Turn bag right side out.

13 Place lining bag pieces together with right sides facing. Pin, baste and stitch from one side point around lower edge to second marked point, taking ¾in (2cm) seam allowance. Turn under ¾in (2cm) along curved top edges; pin and baste.
14 Place nylon lining inside bag with wrong sides together. Place folded edges of lining next to zipper; pin, baste and slip stitch them in place.

T for three

Three cool and comfortable T-shirts to crochet.

Striped top

Sizes
To fit 38[40:42]in (97[102:107]cm) chest.
Length; 27[27½:28½]in (68[69:70]cm).
Sleeve seam, 8½in (21cm).

Note Directions for larger sizes are in brackets [ ]; if there is only one set of figures it applies to all sizes.

Materials
13[13:14]oz (350[350:400]g) of a medium-weight mercerized crochet cotton in main color (A)
7[7:9]oz (200[200:250]g) in 1st contrasting color (B)
6[6:7]oz (150[150:200]g) in 2nd contrasting color (C)
Sizes E and F (3.50 and 4.00mm) crochet hooks

Gauge
18 dc and 10 rows to 4in (10cm) on size F (4.00mm) hook.

Sleeves and yoke section (make 2)
1st size only Using size F (4.00mm) hook and A make 45ch for sleeve edge.
Base row 1dc into 4th ch from hook, 1dc into each ch to end. Turn. 43 sts.
Next row 3ch to count as first dc, 1dc into each dc to end, 1 dc into top of turning ch leaving last 2 loops of last dc on hook, drop A and draw through B. Turn.
Next row 3ch, 1dc into each dc to end. Turn.
Next row 3ch, 1dc into each dc to end leaving last 2 loops of last dc on hook, drop B and draw through A. Turn.
Cont in dc and changing yarns in this way on every other row, work 2 rows A and 2 C.
Beg stripe sequence.
Work 2 rows A, 2 rows B, 2 rows A and 2 rows C until a total of 94 rows has been worked, ending with 2 rows A. Fasten off.
2nd size only Using size F (4.00mm) hook and A, make 47ch for sleeve edge.
Base row Work 1 dc into 4th ch from hook, 1dc into each ch to end leaving last 2 loops of last dc on hook, drop A and draw through B. Turn. 45 sts.
Next row 3ch to count as first dc, 1dc into each dc to end, 1dc into top of 3ch. Turn.
Next row 3ch, 1dc into each dc to end

leaving last 2 loops of last dc on hook, drop B and draw through A. Turn.
Cont in dc and changing yarns in this way on every other row, work 2 rows A and 2 rows C. Now work stripe sequence as for first size until a total of 96 rows has been worked, ending with 1 row A. Fasten off.
3rd size only Using size F (4.00mm) hook and C, make 49ch for sleeve edge.
Base row Work 1dc into 4th ch from hook, 1dc into each ch to end leaving last 2 loops of last dc on hook, drop C and draw through A. Turn. 47 sts.
Next row 3ch to count as first dc, 1dc into each dc to end, 1dc into top of 3ch. Turn.
Next row 3ch, 1dc into each dc to end leaving last 2 loops of last dc on hook, drop A and draw through B. Turn.
Cont in dc and changing yarns in this way on every other row, work 2 rows B, 2 rows A, 2 rows C.
Now work stripe sequence as for first size until a total of 98 rows has been worked, ending with 1 row C. Fasten off.

Lower sections (make 2)
All sizes Using size F (4.00mm) hook and A, make 94[98:102]ch.
Base row Work 1dc into 4th ch from hook, 1dc into each ch to end. Turn.
Next row 3ch to count as first dc, 1dc into each dc to end leaving last 2 loops of last dc on hook, drop A and draw through B. Turn.
Cont in dc and changing yarns in this way on every other row, work 2 rows B, 2 rows A, 2 rows C and 2 rows A until work measures 17½in (44cm) from beg. Fasten off.

To finish
Mark top sections 8½in (21cm) from each sleeve edge. Attach lower sections to top sections between markers. Join side and underarm seams. Join upper sleeve and shoulder seams for 13½in (34cm), so leaving an opening at center for neck.
Using size E (3.50mm) hook and B work a row of sc evenly all around neck. Using size E (3.50mm) hook and B work 1sc into each st around lower and sleeve edges.

Oatmeal top

Sizes

To fit 38[40:42]in (97[102:107]cm chest.
Length, 25½[26:26½]in (64[66:67]cm).
Sleeve seam, 7½in (19cm).

Note Directions for larger sizes are in brackets []; if there is only one set of figures it applies to all sizes.

Materials

15oz (425g) of a lightweight nubbly yarn
Sizes E and F (3.50 and 4.00mm) crochet hooks
Four buttons

Gauge

18dc to 4¼in (11cm) and 11 rows to 4in (10cm) on size F (4.00mm) hook.

Back

Using size F (4.00mm) hook make 87[90:93]ch.

Base row Work 1dc into 4th ch from hook, 1dc into each ch to end. Turn. 85[88:91]sts.
Patt row 3ch to count as first dc, 1dc into first sp between dc, *1dc into next sp between dc, rep from * to end. Turn. Rep patt row until work measures 15½in (39cm) from beg.

Shape armholes

Sl st over first 6 dc, 3ch, patt to within last 5 dc, turn. 75[78:81]dc. Cont straight until armhole measures 8[8½:9]in (20[21.5:23]cm). Change to size E (3.50mm) hook.
Next row 1 ch to count as first sc, working into the top of each dc work 1 sc into each dc to end. Turn. 75[78:91]sc.
Next row 1 ch, 1 sc in each sc to end. Turn. Rep last row until armholes measure 10[10½:11]in (25[27:28]cm).

Shape shoulders

1st row Sl st across first 8[9:9] sts work to within last 7[8:8] sts, turn.
2nd row Sl st across first 8[8:9] sts, work to within last 7[7:8] sts, turn.
3rd row Sl st across first 8 sts, work to within last 7 sts. Fasten off.

Front

Work as given for back until armhole shaping row has been completed. 75[78:81]dc. Work 1 row.

Divide for opening

Next row Work across the first 35[36: 38]dc, turn. 34[35:37] sts. Cont in patt until work measures same as back to beg of sc panel, ending at front edge.

Shape neck

Change to size E (3.50mm) hook.
Next row Sl st across first 8 sts, 1 sc in each st to end. Turn. Cont in sc, dec one st at neck edge on next 7[7:8] rows. Cont straight until front measures same as back to shoulder; end at front edge.

Shape shoulder

Work to within last 7[8:8] sts, turn.
Next row Sl st across first 8[8:9] sts, work to end. Fasten off. Skip 5[6:5] sts at center front, rejoin yarn to next st, then work in patt across the rem 34[35:37] sps, turn. 35[36:38] sts. Cont in patt until work measures as first side to

sc panel; end at armhole edge.

Shape neck

Change to size E (3.50mm) hook.

Next row Work 1 sc in each st to within last 7 sts. Cont in sc, dec one st at neck edge on next 7[7:8] rows. Cont straight until work measures as back to shoulder; end at armhole edge.

Shape shoulder

Sl st across first 8[9:9] sts, work to end. Turn.

Next row Work to within last 7[7:8] sts. Fasten off.

Sleeves

Using size F (4.00mm) hook make, 55[59:63]ch. Change to size E (3.50mm) hook and work 1 sc into 2nd ch from hook, 1 sc into each ch to end. Turn. 54[58:62]sc.

Next row 1 ch, 1 sc in each sc to end. Turn.

Rep last row 4 times more. Change to size F (4.00mm) hook.

Next row 3ch, skip first sc, 1 dc into each sc to end. Turn.

Patt row 3ch to count as first dc, 1 dc into first sp between dc, *1 dc into next sp between dc, rep from * to end. Turn. Cont in patt, inc one st at each end of every foll 4th row until there are 62[66: 70] sts. Cont straight until sleeve measures 7in (18cm) from beg. Mark each end of last row with a colored thread.

Work 3 rows without shaping.

Shape top

Next row Sl st across first 4dc, 3ch, (1 dc into next sp) to within last 3 sps, turn. Rep last row until 8[6:4] sts rem. Fasten off.

Button band

Join shoulder seams.

Using size E (3.50mm) hook join on yarn and work 6sc along lower edge of front opening.

Next row 1 ch, 1 sc into each sc to end. Turn.

Rep last row until band fits along opening to beg of neck shaping, when slightly stretched, ending at front edge. Fasten off. Mark 3 button positions on this band, the first 1½in (4cm) from base of opening the last 1½in (4cm) from the top and the other one evenly spaced between.

Buttonhole band

Working in front of and on top of button band work a sc into each of same 6 places as 6sc of button band. Now cont in sc work to match button band making buttonholes to correspond as foll:

1st buttonhole row 1 ch, 1 sc into each of the first 2sc, 2ch skip next 2sc, 1 sc into each of last 2sc. Turn.

2nd buttonhole row 1 ch, 1 sc into each of the first 2sc, 1 sc into each of the 2ch, then work 1 sc into each of the last 2sc. Turn. Do not fasten off.

Neckband

Work across buttonhole band, then work 1 sc into each of the sts of left front neck, 1 sc into each row end up side neck, 1 sc into each sp between dc on back neck, 1 sc into each row end down right side neck, 1 sc into each st along right front neck and 1 sc into each of the 6sc of button band. Work 5 rows in sc working a buttonhole over the 3rd and 4th rows. Fasten off.

To finish

Sew front bands in position. Join side and sleeve seams, leaving 3 rows above markers on sleeves open. Set in sleeves, placing 3 rows above markers to armhole shaping. Sew on buttons. Press or block according to yarn used.

Rustic top

Sizes

To fit 38[40:42]in (97[102:107]cm) chest.

Length, 25[25½:26]in (63[64:65]cm).

Sleeve seam, 4½in (11cm).

Note Directions for larger sizes are in brackets []; if there is only one set of figures it applies to all sizes.

Materials

17[18:19]oz (340[360:380]g) of a sport yarn

Sizes C and E (3.00 and 3.50mm) crochet hooks

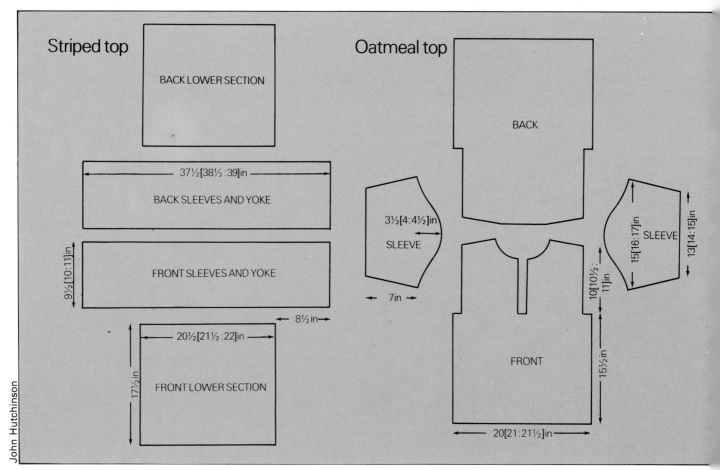

Gauge

10 patterns measure 4¼in (10.5cm) using size E (3.50mm) hook.

Back

Using size E (3.50mm) hook make 101[105:109]ch.

Base row Work (1sc and 1dc) into 3rd ch from hook, *skip next ch, (1sc and 1dc) into next ch, rep from * to end. Turn. 50[52:54] patts.

Patt row 1ch, *skip next dc, (1sc and 1dc) into next sc, rep from * to end. The last row forms the patt and is rep throughout. Cont in patt until back measures 13½in (34cm). Do not turn.

Shape sleeves

Make 13ch at end of last row. Turn.

Next row Work 1sc into 3rd ch from hook, 1dc into same ch, (skip 1ch, 1sc and 1dc into next ch) 5 times, patt across sts for back. Using a separate ball of yarn, sl st into last st of previous row and make 12ch. Fasten off. Return to end of row just worked and cont to work across additional ch, (skip next ch, 1sc and 1dc into next ch) 6 times. 62[64:66] patts. **

Cont straight until sleeve measures 6¼[6¾:6¾]in (16[17:17]cm); end with WS row.

Yoke detail

***Next row** 2ch, work 1hdc into each st to end. Turn.

Next row 2ch, working into front loop

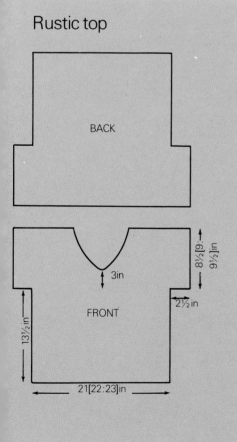

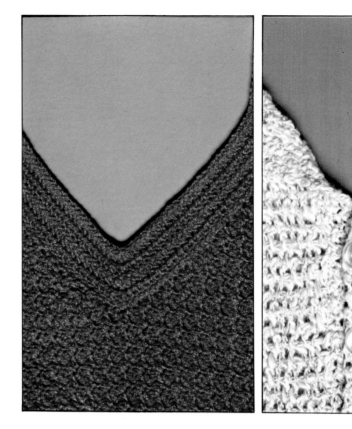

only of each st, work 1hdc into each st to end. Turn.***

Next row 1ch, *skip 1hdc, work (1sc and 1hdc) into next hdc, rep from * to end. Turn. 62[64:66] patts.

Cont straight until sleeve measures 8½[9:9½]in (22[23:24]cm). Fasten off.

Waistband

With RS facing and using size C (3.00mm) hook, rejoin yarn at lower edge of back. Work 3ch, then work 1hdc into each remaining loop on foundation ch. Turn. 100[104:108]hdc.

Working into front loop only of each st, work 10 more rows hdc. Fasten off.

Front

Work as for back to **. Cont straight until sleeve measures 3in (7.5cm) from beg, end with WS row.

Shape neck

Next row 1ch, work 30[31:32] patts, skip 1dc, 1sc into next sc, turn and leave rem 31[32:33] patts unworked.

Next row 1ch, skip first sc and next dc, work (1sc and 1dc) into next sc, patt to end. Turn.

Next row Work in patt until one patt rem unworked, skip next dc, 1sc into last sc. Turn.

****Rep last 2 rows until sleeve measures 6¼[6¾:6¾]in (16[17:17]cm); end with WS row.

Work as for back from *** to ***, dec 1hdc by skipping one st at neck edge on every row. Cont to shape neck as before, until 22[22:23] patts rem. Cont

straight until sleeve measures same as sleeves of back. Fasten off. With RS of work facing, rejoin yarn to next dc at center front, work (1sc and 1dc) into next sc, patt to end. Turn.

Next row Work in patt until 1 patt rem unworked, skip next dc, work 1sc into last sc. Turn.

Next row 1ch, skip first sc and next dc, work (1sc and 1dc) into next sc, patt to end. Turn.

Rep last 2 rows. Now work as for first side from **** to end.

Waistband

Work as for back.

To finish

Press or block according to yarn used. Join shoulder seams.

Neck border

With RS facing and using size C (3.00mm) hook, rejoin yarn at left shoulder and work 44[47:50]sc down left side of front neck, place a marker after last sc for center front V, work 44[47:50]sc up right side of neck and 37[41:41]sc along back neck. Turn. 125[135:141]sc. Work 4 rows hdc as for waistband, working 2hdc tog at each side of marker on every row. Fasten off. Sew ends of neck border tog.

Sleeve borders

With RS facing and using size C (3.00mm) hook, rejoin yarn to lower edge of sleeve and work 92[98:104]sc along this edge. Work 8 rows hdc as for waistband. Fasten off.

Finish other sleeve in the same way. Join side and underarm seams. Press lightly.

Rustic top

BACK

FRONT

8½[9:9½]in

3in

2½in

13½in

21[22:23]in

from * to end omitting 2sc at end of last rep, sl st into first ch. 40 sts.
6th round 1ch, *2sc into next sc, 1sc into each of next 3 sts, rep from * to end omitting 1sc at end of last rep, sl st into first ch. 50 sts.
7th round 1ch, *1sc into next sc, 2sc into next sc, 1sc into each of next 3sc, rep from * to end omitting 1sc at end of last rep, sl st into first ch. 60 sts.
8th round 1ch, 1sc into each of next 4sc, *1tr around previous tr, 1sc into each of next 5sc, rep from * to end omitting 5sc at end of last rep, sl st into first ch.

Top hats

If you want to get ahead . . . crochet a hat, or two, or all three of these super toppers. Add a lacy scarf and you're guaranteed winter warmth.

Hat with rolled brim and triangular scarf

Size
Hat to fit average head.
Scarf depth at center, 16½in (42cm).

Materials
Hat *5oz (140g) of a knitting worsted, or mohair-type yarn of similar weight*
Scarf *3oz (75g) of a knitting worsted*
Size H (5.50mm) crochet hook

Gauge
Hat 11sc to 4in (10cm) worked on size H (5.50mm) hook.
Scarf 3 patts to 5in (13cm) worked on size H (5.50mm) hook.

Hat

Using size H (5.50mm) hook make 4ch, sl st into first ch to form a ring.
1st round 1ch, now work 9sc into ring, sl st into first ch.
2nd round 1ch, *2sc into next sc, 1sc into next sc, rep from * to end, finishing 2sc into last sc, sl st into first ch.
3rd round 1ch, *2sc into next sc, 1sc into each of next 2sc, rep from * to end, sl st into first ch. 20 sts.
4th round 1ch, *2sc into next sc, 1sc into next sc, rep from * to end, sl st into first ch. 30 sts.
5th round 1ch, 1sc into same place as last sl st, *1sc into next sc, (yo) twice, insert hook into the horizontal loop of next sc 3 rows below, yo and complete tr in the usual way, 2sc into next sc, rep

9th round 1 ch, 1 sc into each st to end, sl st into first ch.
10th round As 9th.
Rep 8th–10th rounds until work measures 8 in (20 cm).
Now cont in rounds of sc only until work measures 11 in (28 cm). Fasten off.
Roll back sc rounds tightly to form brim.

Scarf

Using size H (5.50mm) hook make 181 ch.
Base row 4dc into 4th ch from hook, *skip next 2ch, 1dc into next ch, skip next 2ch, 5dc into next ch, rep from * to within last 3ch, skip next 2ch, sl st into last ch.
Turn. 30 shells.
Next row 3ch, 1sc into center dc of first shell, *1 shell into next single dc, 1dc into center dc of next shell, rep from * to within last shell, sl st into center dc of next shell, turn. 29 shells.
Rep last row working 1 shell less on every row until 1 shell rem. Fasten off.
Join yarn to foundation ch and work 3sc into each 2ch sp. Fasten off.

Victor Yuan

Motif hat

Size
To fit average head.

Materials
*3oz (60g) of a sport yarn in each of
2 contrasting colors (A and B)
Size F (4.00mm) crochet hook*

Gauge
18sc to 4in (10cm) worked on size F
(4.00mm) hook.

Ear pieces (make 2)
Using size F (4.00mm) hook and A,
make 7ch.
Base row 1sc into 3rd ch from hook, 1sc
into each of next 3ch, 3sc into last ch, then
work 1sc into each rem loop on other
side of foundation ch. Turn. Join on B.
Next row With B, work 2ch to count as
first sc, 1sc into each of next 5sc, 4sc into
end sc, 1sc into each of next 6sc. Turn.
Next row With B, work 2ch to count as
first sc, 1sc into each of next 5sc, work
2sc into each of the 4sc at point, 1sc into
each of next 6sc. Turn.
Next row With A, work 2ch to count as
first sc, 1sc into each of next 7sc, 2sc
into each of next 4sc at point, 1sc into
each of next 8sc. Turn.
Next row With A, work 2ch to count as
first sc, 1sc into each of next 10sc, 2sc
into each of next 2sc at point, 1sc into
each of next 11sc. Turn. Inc in the 2sc
at point on every row, as before, work 2
rows B and 2 rows A. 34sc.
Cont in sc work in 2-color patt, weaving
yarn across row, as folls:
Next row Work 5B, 5A, 5B, 1A, with A
work 2sc into next sc, with B work 1sc
into same place as last sc, with A work
2sc into next sc, 1A, 5B, 5A and 5B.
Turn. 37sc.
Next row 5B, 5A, 5B, 2A, with A work
2sc into next sc, with B work 3sc into
next sc, with A work 2sc, into next sc,
2A, 5B, 5A and 5B. Turn. 41sc.
Next row 5B, 5A, 5B, 3A, with A work
2sc into next sc, 1B, with B work 3sc
into next sc, 1B, with A work 2sc into
next sc, 3A, 5B, 5A, 5B. Turn. 45sc.
Next row (5B, 5A) twice, 2B, with B
work 3sc into next sc, 2B, (5A, 5B)

twice. Turn. 47sc.
Next row (5B, 5A) twice, 3B, with B
work 3sc into next sc, 3B, (5A, 5B)
twice. Fasten off. 49sc.
Main piece
Using size F (4.00mm) hook and B, make
10ch, then work 29sc across top of one
ear piece, 22ch, work 29sc across top of
other ear piece, 10ch, sl st into first ch to
form a ring.
Next round 1ch, 1sc into each ch and sc
to end, sl st into first ch. 100 sts.
Working in sc, work 1 round A, 1 round
B and 4 rounds A.
Now foll the chart and weaving yarn
across the row, work 17 rows.
Work 1 round B.
Shape top
Next round With B, work *1sc into each
of next 8sc, work next 2sc tog, rep from
* to end, sl st into first sc. 90sc.
Next round With B, work 1sc into each
sc to end, sl st into first sc.
Next round With B, work *1sc into each
of next 7sc, work next 2sc tog, rep from
* to end, sl st into first sc. 80sc.
Next round With B, work 1 sc into each sc
* to end, sl st into first sc.
Next round With A, work *1sc into each
of next 6sc, work next 2sc tog, rep from
* to end, sl st into first sc. 70sc.
Next round With A, work 1sc into each
sc to end, sl st into first sc.
Next round With A, work *1sc into each
of next 5sc, work next 2sc tog, rep from
* to end, sl st into first sc. 60sc.
Next round With A, work 1sc into each
sc to end, sl st into first sc.
Next round With B, work 1sc into each
of next 4sc, work next 2sc tog, rep from
* to end, sl st into first sc. 50sc.
Next round With B, work 1sc into each of
next 3sc, work next 2sc tog, rep from
* to end, sl st into first sc. 40sc.
Next round With B, work 1sc into each of
next 2sc, work next 2sc tog, rep from
* to end, sl st into first sc. 30sc.

Next round With A, work *1sc into next
sc, work next 2sc tog, rep from * to end,
sl st into first sc. 20sc.
Next round With A, *work next 2sc tog,
rep from * to end, sl st into first sc. 10sc.
Cut off yarn leaving a long end, thread
end through last 10sc, draw up tightly
and secure.
Using one strand of each color together,
make 2 twisted cords and sew one cord
to the point of each ear piece.

Rolled-brim hat

Size
To fit average head.

Materials
*4oz (100g) of a knitting worsted
Size H (5.50mm) crochet hook*

Gauge
11sc to 4in (10cm) worked on size H
(5.50mm) hook.
To make
Work as for rolled-brim hat with scarf; do
not make scarf.

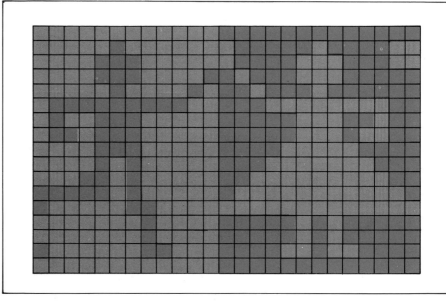

John Hutchinson

EXTRA SPECIAL KNITTING

Two's company

The simple patterns on this man's pullover are echoed in the textured patterns on the jacket.

Sizes

To fit 36[38:40:42]in (92[97:102: 107]cm) chest.
Pullover length, 24[24:25½:25½]in (61[61:64:64]cm).
Jacket length, 29[29:29½:29½]in (74[74:75:75]cm).
Sleeve seam, 19in (48cm).
Note Directions for larger sizes are in brackets []; if there is only one set of figures it applies to all sizes.

Materials

Pullover
11[11:11:13]oz (300[300:300: 350]g) of a fingering yarn in main color (A)
4oz (100g) in each of two contrasting colors (B and C)
1 pair each Nos. 2, 3 and 4 (3, 3¼ and 3¾mm) knitting needles
Jacket
18[20:20:22]oz (500[550:550: 600]g) of a knitting worsted in main color (A)
13[15:15:15]oz (350[400:400: 400]g) in 1st contrasting color (B)
11[11:11:13]oz (300[300:300: 350]g) in 2nd contrasting color (C)
1 pair each Nos. 5, 6 and 7 (4, 4½ and 5mm) knitting needles
6 buttons

Gauge

Pullover 28st and 32 rows to 4in (10cm) in main patt using No. 4 (3¾mm) needles.
Jacket 18 sts and 22 rows to 4in (10cm) in stockinette st using No. 7 (5mm) needles.

Pullover

Back

Using No. 2 (3mm) needles and A, cast on 134[142:150:158] sts.
1st ribbing row P2, (K2, P2) to end.
2nd ribbing row K2, (P2, K2) to end.
Rep these 2 rows for 4in (10cm); end with a 2nd ribbing row and dec one st at end of last row. 133[141:149:157] sts.
Change to No. 4 (3¾mm) needles. Join on B. Beg main patt.
1st row (RS) K with A.
2nd row P with A.
3rd row K1 A, (1 B, 3A) to end.
4th row P with A.

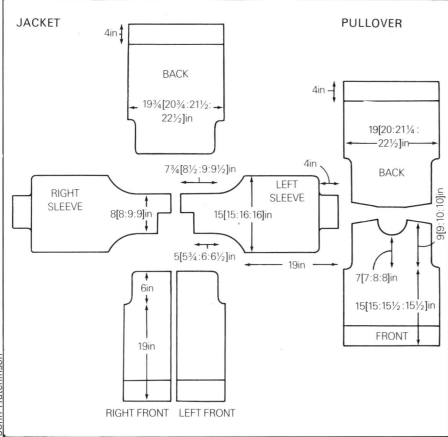

JACKET

4in

BACK

19¾[20¾:21½: 22½]in

PULLOVER

4in

19[20:21¼: 22½]in

BACK

4in

7¾[8½:9:9½]in

RIGHT SLEEVE

LEFT SLEEVE

8[8:9:9]in

15[15:16:16]in

5[5¾:6:6½]in

19in

FRONT

7[7:8:8]in

15[15:15½:15½]in

9[9:10:10]in

6in

19in

RIGHT FRONT LEFT FRONT

John Hutchinson

5th row K with A.
6th row P1 A (1 B, 3 A) to end.
These 6 rows form patt. Cont in patt until work measures 15[15:15½:15½]in (38[38:39:39]cm); end with a WS row.

Shape armholes
Keeping patt correct, bind off 8 sts at beg of next 2 rows. Dec one st at each end of next and every foll alternate row until 109[113:117:121] sts rem. Cont straight until armhole measures 4[4:4¾:4¾]in (10[10:12:12]cm); end with a 2nd or 4th row.*
Yoke
Change to No. 3 (3¼mm) needles and work in garter st, working in stripes of 2 rows C and 2 rows B until armhole measures 9[9:10:10]in (23[23:25: 25]cm); end WS.
Shape shoulders
Bind off 11[11:12:12] sts at beg of next 4 rows and 11[12:11:12] sts at beg of foll 2 rows. Cut off yarn and leave rem 43[45:47:49] sts on a holder.

Front
Work as for back to *
Yoke
Change to No. 3 (3¼mm) needles and work in garter st, working in stripes of 2 rows C and 2 rows B until armhole measures 7[7:8:8]in (18[18:20:20]cm); end WS.
Divide for neck
Next row K38[39:40:41], turn and leave

rem sts on a spare needle.
Complete left side of neck first. Dec one st at neck edge on every row until 33[34:35:36] sts rem. Cont straight until armhole measures 9[9:10:10]in (23[23:25:25]cm); end at armhole edge.
Shape shoulder
Bind off 11[11:12:12] sts at beg of next and foll alternate row. Work 1 row. Bind off. Return to sts that were left. With RS facing place next 33[35:37:39] sts on a holder, join yarn to next st and K to end of row. Complete to match first side reversing shaping.

Neckband
Join right shoulder seam. With RS facing, using No. 2 (3mm) needles join A to top of left front neck and pick up and K 21 sts from left front neck, K sts from holder, pick up and K 21 sts from right front neck, then K back neck sts from holder. 118[122:126:130] sts. Beg with a 2nd ribbing row, rib as for back for 2in (5cm). Bind off in ribbing.

Armhole borders (alike)
Join left shoulder and neckband seam. With RS facing, using No. 2 (3mm) needles and A, pick up and K 142[142: 150:150] sts evenly along armhole edge. Beg with a 2nd ribbing row, rib as for back for 1in (2.5cm). Bind off in ribbing.

To finish
Press or block according to yarn used.

Join side seams. Fold neckband under to WS and slip stitch in place.

Jacket

Back
Using No. 5 (4mm) needles and A, cast on 90[94:98:102] sts.
1st ribbing row P2, (K2, P2) to end.
2nd ribbing row K2, (P2, K2) to end.
Rep these 2 rows for 4in (10cm); end with a 2nd ribbing row and dec one st at at end of last row. 89[93:97:101] sts. Change to No. 7 (5mm) needles. Beg garter st patt.
1st and 2nd rows K with B.
3rd and 4th rows K with C.
5th and 6th rows K with B.
These 6 rows form garter st patt.
Beg dotted patt.
1st row K with A.
2nd row P with A.
3rd row K2 A, 1 C, (3A, 1C) to last 2 sts, 2A.
4th row P with A.
5th row K with A.
6th row P (1 C, 3A) to last st, 1C.
These 6 rows form dotted patt. Rep them three times more. With A, K1 row and P1 row. Work 6 rows of garter st patt once and 6 rows of dotted patt 4 times. With A, K1 row and P1 row. Now work 6 rows of garter st patt again.
Beg bobble patt.
1st–4th rows With C, work in stockinette st.
5th row K4[6:8:2] C, (with B, work K1, P1, K1, P1 and K1 all into next st, turn, P5, turn, K5, turn, P5 turn K5, then pass 4th, 3rd, 2nd and 1st sts over 5th st– bobble made or MB, K7 C) to last 5[7:9:3] sts, MB with B, K4 [6:8:2] C.
6th–10th rows With C, work in stockinette st.
11th row K8 [2:4:6], (MB with B, K7 C) to last 9[3:5:7] sts, MB with B, K8[2:4:6] C.
12th–16th rows With C, work in stockinette st.
17th row As 5th row.
18th–22nd rows With C, work in stockinette st. These 22 rows form the bobble patt.
Shape armholes
Working in garter st patt, bind off 4 sts at beg of next 2 rows. Dec one st at each end of next and foll alternate row. Work 1 row. Working in spotted patt, dec one st at each end of next and every foll alternate row until 73[77:81:85] sts rem. Cont straight until the 3rd dotted patt rep has been worked. With A, K1 row and P1 row. Working in garter st patt, dec one st at each end of every row. 61[65:69:73] sts. With C, bind off.

Pocket linings (make 2)
Using No. 7 (5mm) needles and A, cast on 20 sts. Work 32 rows stockinette st;

90

end with a P row. Cut off yarn and leave sts on a holder.

Left front
Using No. 5 (4mm) needles and A, cast on 46[46:50:50] sts.
Rib as for back for 4in (10cm); end with a 2nd ribbing row and dec one st at end of last row on 1st and 3rd sizes and inc one st at end of last row on 2nd and 4th sizes. 45[47:49:51] sts. Change to No. 7 (5mm) needles. Work garter st patt as for back.
Beg dotted patt.
1st row K with A.
2nd row P with A.
3rd row K2 A, 1 C, (3A, 1 C) to last 2[0:2:0] sts, 2[0:2:0] A.
4th row P with A.
5th row K with A.
6th row P0[2:0:2] A, 1 C, (3A, 1 C) to end.
These 6 rows form dotted patt. Rep them three times. With A, K1 row and P1 row. Work 6 rows garter st patt.

Divide for pocket
Next row K12[13:14:15] A, with B, bind off 20, K13[14:15:16] A.
Next row P13[14:15:16] A, P the sts of one pocket lining, P to end of row.
Cont in dotted patt until the 4th dotted patt rep has been worked. With A, K1 row and P1 row. Work garter st patt. Work bobble patt as for back but work bobble rows thus:
5th row K4[6:8:2] C, MB with B, (K7 C, MB with B) to end.
11th row K8[2:4:6] C, MB with B, (K7 C, MB with B) to last 4 sts, K4 C.

Shape armhole
Working in garter st patt, bind off 4 sts at beg of next row. Dec one st at beg of foll 2 alternate rows. Work 1 row. Working in dotted patt, dec one st at beg of next and every foll alternate row until 37[39:41:43] sts rem. Cont without shaping until the 3rd dotted patt rep has been worked. With A, K1 row and P1 row. Working in garter st patt, dec one st at armhole edge on every row. 31[33:35:37] sts. With C, bind off.

Right front
Work as for left front reversing shaping and reading patt rows from end to beg.

Left sleeve
Using No. 5 (4mm) needles and A, cast on 34[34:38:38] sts. Work ribbing rows 1 and 2 of back for 4in (10cm); end with a 2nd ribbing row and for 1st and 2nd sizes only inc one st at end of last row. Join on B.
Next row With B, K0[0:2:2], (K twice in next st) to last st, K1. 69[69:73:73] sts. K1 row B, 2 rows C and 2 rows B.
Work dotted patt as for back 4 times. With A, K 1 row and P 1 row. Work garter st patt as for back. Rep from * to * once more. Now work bobble patt as for back following 2nd [2nd:3rd:3rd] size.

Shape top
Working in garter st patt, bind off 4 sts at beg of next 2 rows. Work 4 rows. Working in dotted patt, dec one st at each end of next and every foll alternate row until 37[37:41:41] sts rem. Work 1 row. Now with A, K 1 row and P 1 row dec one st at each end of first row. 35[35:39:39] sts.

Saddle shoulder extension
Cont straight working in stripes of 2 rows B and 2 rows C until saddle shoulder extension measures 5[5¾:6:6½]in (13[14.5:15:16.5]cm); end with a RS row.

Shape neck
Cont in stripes, bind off 18[18:20:20] sts at beg of next row. Cont in stripes for a further 2¾[2¾:3:3]in (7[7:7.5:7.5]cm) for back neck; end with a WS row. Bind off.

Right sleeve
Work as for left sleeve, reversing neck shaping.

Collar
Join bound-off edge of sleeves tog for center back. Join saddle shoulder extensions to top of fronts, leaving 12[12:13:13] sts free at front edge. With RS facing, join B to right front neck and using No. 5 (4mm) needles pick up and K 12[13:13:14] sts from right front neck, 18[18:20:20] sts from sleeve, 24[26:26:28] sts across back neck, 18[18:20:20] sts from sleeve and 12[13:13:14] sts from left front neck. 84[88:92:96] sts.
1st ribbing row K2, (P2, K2) to end.
2nd ribbing row K1, P1, (K2, P2) to last 2 sts, P1, K1.
Rep these 2 rows for 2in (5cm). Change to No. 6 (4½mm) needles and work a further 2in (5cm). Change to No. 7 (5mm) needles and cont in ribbing until collar measures 6in (15cm) from beg. Bind off loosely in ribbing.

Button border
Using No. 5 (4mm) needles and B, cast on 6 sts. Work in garter st until band, slightly stretched, fits along front edge to neck. Bind off.
Sew on border. Mark 6 button positions on this border, the first ½in (1cm) from lower edge and the others level with bands of garter st patt.

Buttonhole border
Work as for button border but make buttonholes to correspond with markers as foll:
1st buttonhole row K2, bind off 2, K2.
2nd buttonhole row K2, bind on 2, K2.

To finish
Block; depending on yarn used, press dotted patt only. Join top edge of back to saddle shoulder extensions. Sew sleeves to armholes, then join side and sleeve seams. Sew down pocket linings. Sew on buttonhole border and buttons.

KNITTING

Double take

Use of texture and tweedy yarns gives these sweaters an outdoor look.

Sizes

To fit 32[34:36:38:40:42]in (83[87:92:97:102:107]cm) chest.
Length, 24[24:24:27:27:27]in (61[61:61:69:69:69]cm).
Sleeve seam, 19[19¼:19¼:21:21¾:21¾]in (48[49:49:53:55:55]cm).
Note Directions for larger sizes are in brackets []; if there is only one set of figures it applies to all sizes.

Materials

11[11:13:13:15:15]oz (300[300: 350:350:400:400]g) of a tweed-textured yarn in knitting worsted weight in 1st color (A)
4[4:6:6:8:8]oz (100[100:150:150: 200:200]g) in 2nd color (B)
7[7:9:9:11:11]oz (200[200:250: 250:300:300]g) in 3rd color (C)
6oz (150g) in 4th color (D)
1 pair each Nos. 5 and 7 (4 and 5mm) knitting needles
Set of 4 double-pointed needles: No. 5 (4mm) for V-neck sweater; No. 7 (5mm) for turtleneck

Gauge

18 sts and 24 rows to 4in (10cm) in reverse stockinette st on No. 7 (5mm) needles.

V-neck sweater

Back and front (worked in one piece)
**Using No. 7 (5mm) needles and A[C:B:C:D:A], cast on 180[180:180:208:208:208] sts for entire left side edge. P 1 row and K 1 row.
Join on colors as required and beg with P row, cont in patt working 2 rows stockinette st and 2 rows reverse stockinette st as foll:
For 2nd size only, work 2 rows A.
For 3rd size only, work 2 rows C and 2 rows A.
For 4th size only, work 2 rows A, 2 rows B, 2 rows C and 2 rows A.
For 5th size only, work 2 rows C, 2 rows A, 2 rows B, 2 rows C and 2 rows A.
For all sizes, work 2 rows D, 2 rows C, 2 rows A, 2 rows B, 2 rows C and 2 rows A.
Last 12 rows form stripe patt. Cont in patt,

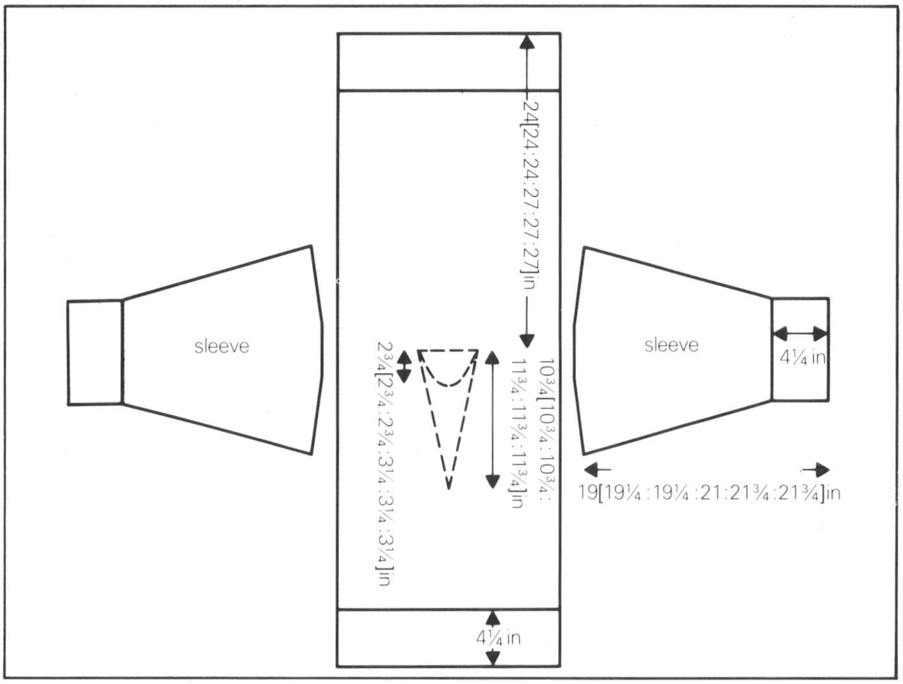
sleeve
sleeve
4¼ in
19[19¼:19¼:21:21¾:21¾]in
24[24:24:27:27:27]in
10¾[10¾:10¾:11¾:11¾:11¾]in
2¾[2¾:2¾:3¼:3¼:3¼]in
4¼ in

Brian Mayor

work [24:24:22:22:34] rows.

Divide for back

Next row Patt 90[90:90:104:104:104], turn and leave rem sts on a spare needle for front. Cont on first set of sts for back. Work 3[3:3:5:5:5] rows. Now work (4 rows A and 2 rows D) 3 times, 4 rows A and 2 rows C.

For 1st, 2nd and 3rd sizes only, work 1 row D.

For 4th, 5th and 6th sizes only, work 2 rows D and 1 row A.

For all sizes, cut off yarns and leave sts on a spare needle.**

With RS of work facing rejoin D[D:D:A:A:A] to inner end of front sts on spare needle, bind off 22 sts, work to end.

Next row Work to end.

Next row Using C[C:C:D:D:D], bind off 4, work to end. 64[64:64:78:78:78] sts.

Next row Work to end.

For 4th, 5th and 6th sizes only, using C, bind off 4, work to end. 74 sts.

Next row Work to end.

For all sizes, binding off 4 sts at beg of next row and every alternate row, work 4 rows A, 2 rows D, 4 rows A and 1 row D. 40[40:40:50:50:50] sts. Casting on 4 sts at end of next row and every alternate row, work 1 row D, 4 rows A, 2 rows D, 4 rows A and 2 rows C. 68[68:68:78:78:78] sts.

Next row With D work to end.

For 4th, 5th and 6th sizes only, work to end, turn and cast on 4 sts. 82 sts.

Next row With A, work to end.

For all sizes, with D[D:D:A:A:A], work to end, cast on 22, then onto same needle patt back sts from spare needle 180[180:180:208:208:208] sts.

For 1st, 2nd and 3rd sizes only, with A, work 2 rows.

For all sizes, work 2 rows C, 2 rows B, 2 rows A, 2 rows C, 2 rows D and 2 rows A. The last 12 rows form stripe patt. Cont in patt, work 24[26:28:32:34:36] rows. With A[C:B:C:D:A], bind off.

Waistbands (back and front alike)

With RS of work facing, using No. 5 (4mm) needles and A, pick up and K 77[81:85:91:95:99] sts evenly along lower edge.

1st row (WS) K1, *P1, K1, rep from *.

2nd row K2, *P1, K1, rep from * to last st, K1. Rep these 2 rows 9 times more. Work first row again. Bind off in ribbing.

Sleeves

Using No. 5 (4mm) needles and A, cast on 39[39:39:47:47:47] sts. Beg with 2nd row, work 2 ribbing rows of waistbands 11 times. Change to No. 7 (5mm) needles and cont in patt as for back and front, working in stripe patt of 2 rows A, 2 B, 2 C, 2 A, 2 D and 2 C throughout but inc one st at each end of 3rd and every foll 4th row until there are 71[71:71:79:79:79] sts. Cont straight until sleeve measures 19[19¼:19¼:21:21¾:21¾)in (48[49:49:53:55:55]cm); end with WS row.

Shape top

Bind off 7[7:7:9:9:9] sts at beg of next 2 rows and 8[8:8:9:9:9] sts at beg of foll 4 rows. Bind off rem 25 sts.

Neckband

With RS facing, using set of No. 5 (4mm) needles and A, onto first needle pick up and K 25[25:25:27:27:27] sts across back neck, onto 2nd needle pick up and K 51[51:51:55:55:55] sts along left front neck, onto 3rd needle pick up and K one st from center front and mark this st with colored thread, then pick up and K 51[51:51:55:55:55] sts along right side of neck. 128[128:128:138:138:138] sts. Work 10 rounds in K1, P1 ribbing, dec one st at each side of marked st. Bind off in ribbing dec as before.

To finish

Mark center of bound-off edge of sleeves with pin, matching pin to center of side edge of body. Sew sleeves to back and front. Join side and sleeve seams.

Turtleneck sweater

Back and front (worked in one piece)

Work as for V-neck sweater from ** to **. With RS facing rejoin D[D:D:A:A:A] to inner end of front sts on spare needle, bind off 6, work to end.

Next row Work to end.

Next row Using C[C:C:D:D:D], bind off 2, work to end. 82[82:82:96:96:96] sts.

For 4th, 5th and 6th sizes only, with C, bind off 2, work to end. 94 sts.

Next row Work to end.

For all sizes, binding off 2 sts at beg of next and every foll alternate row work 4 rows A and 2 D. 76[76:76:88:88:88] sts. Cont straight, work 4 rows A, 2 D, 4 A and 1 D. Casting on 2 sts at end of next row and every foll alternate row work 1 row D, 4 A, and 2 C. 84[84:84:96:96:96] sts.

For 4th, 5th and 6th sizes only, work 1 row with D.

Next row Work to end, cast on 2 sts. 98 sts.

For all sizes, work 1 row with D[D:D:A:A:A].

Next row Work to end, cast on 6. Onto same needle patt back sts from spare needle. 180[180:180:208:208:208] sts.

For 1st, 2nd and 3rd sizes only, work 2 rows with A.

For all sizes, work 2 rows C, 2 B, 2 A, 2 C, 2 D and 2 A. Last 12 rows form stripe patt. Cont in patt work 24[26:28:32:34:36] rows. Using A[C:B:C:D:A], bind off.

Waistbands (back and front alike)

Work as for V-neck sweater.

Sleeves

Work as sleeves of V-neck sweater.

Turtleneck

With RS facing, using set of No. 7 (5mm) needles and A, onto first needle pick up and K 30[30:30:34:34:34] sts across back neck, onto 2nd needle pick up and K 21[21:21:23:23:23] sts along left front neck to center front, then onto 3rd needle pick up and K 21[21:21:23:23:23] sts across remainder of center front neck and along right front neck. 72[72:72:80:80:80] sts. Work in K1, P1 ribbing for 7[7:7:9:9:9]in (18[18:18:23:23:23]cm). Bind off very loosely in ribbing.

To finish

As for V-neck sweater. Fold collar to right side.

Sail set

These unisex terrycloth tops are perfect for the active life.

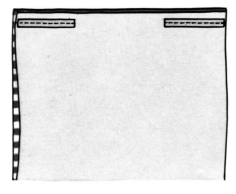

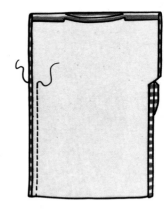

Measurements
To fit sizes 10 to 16 (small to medium men's sizes).
Finished length 28½in (72cm).

Note ⅝in (1.5cm) seam allowances are included throughout.
Measurements for larger sizes are given in brackets [] : where only one figure is given, it applies to all sizes.

Suggested fabric
The tops should be made in stretch terrycloth.

Materials
3yd (2.7m) of 36in (90cm)-wide stretch terrycloth (all sizes)
½yd (.4m) of matching seam binding
2¾yd (2.5m) cotton cord
Matching thread
Yardstick

1 Cut out the fabric pieces following the appropriate measurement diagram and cutting layout. On back and front pieces mark the shoulder and underarm points, and mark center front of lower edge with tailor's tacks. Mark a line down the center of all the pocket pieces with basting stitches.

2 Cut two pieces of seam binding the length of the shoulder seam: 5¼[5⅞:6¼: 7]in (13.5[15:16:17.5]cm). With right sides together and raw edges even, place back and front shoulder seams together. Center seam binding along seamline. Pin, baste and stitch shoulder seams through all layers. (Binding prevents fabric from stretching.) Press seams open. Do not clip neck edges, but press down seam allowance along neck edge.

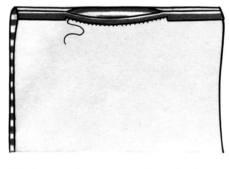

3 Roll seam allowances under on back and front neck and catch-stitch in place.

4 With right sides together and raw edges even stitch side seams. Press seams open and finish. Clip into seam allowance at underarm and finish. Sew sleeve seams. Finish seam allowances (see Technique tip, page 98).

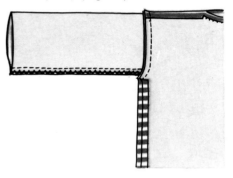

5 With right sides together and underarm seams matching, pin, baste and stitch the sleeves to the armholes. Press the seam allowances toward the sleeves. Turn the top right side out.

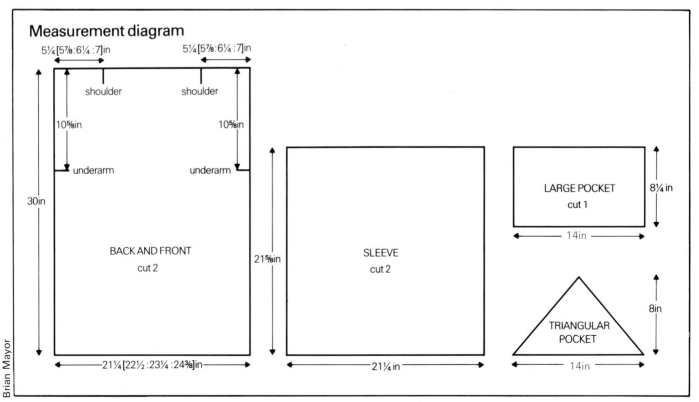

Measurement diagram

5¼[5⅞:6¼ :7]in   5¼[5⅞:6¼ :7]in

shoulder   shoulder

10⅝in   10⅝in

underarm   underarm

30in

BACK AND FRONT
cut 2

21¼[22½ :23¼ :24⅜]in

21⅝in

SLEEVE
cut 2

21¼in

LARGE POCKET
cut 1

8¼in

14in

TRIANGULAR
POCKET

8in

14in

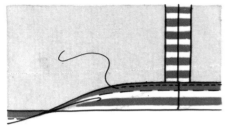

6 Turn under a $\frac{1}{4}$in (6mm) hem at the lower edge and baste. Turn up a further $\frac{5}{8}$in (1.5cm) and stitch close to the fold to form a casing for the drawstring. Repeat for sleeves at both wrists.

7 Cut a $\frac{3}{8}$in (1cm) slit at center front of hem casing. Roll under raw edges and blanket stitch firmly in place. Repeat for wrist casings, making the slits opposite the underarm seams.

Terry Evans

Kim Sayer

Cutting layout (for all sizes) 36in-wide fabric

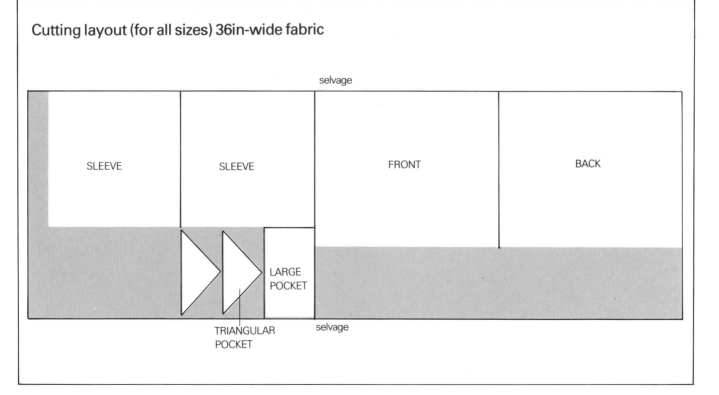

selvage

| SLEEVE | SLEEVE | FRONT | BACK |

LARGE POCKET

TRIANGULAR POCKET

selvage

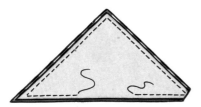

8 With right sides together, pin, baste and stitch the two triangular pocket pieces together, leaving 2in (5cm) open along lower edge and taking $\frac{5}{8}$in (1.5cm) seams. Clip the corners and turn right side out. Turn in seam allowances along the opening at the lower edge and slip stitch neatly to close.

9 Turn under a $\frac{3}{4}$in (2cm) hem along one long edge of large pocket. Topstitch with two lines of stitching. Turn under and baste seam allowances on remaining sides.
10 Place the triangular pocket on the large pocket, aligning bases and center lines. Pin and baste in place.

11 Place the large pocket on the front of the garment, matching lower edges of pockets to the stitching line of hem and aligning the center fronts. Topstitch both pockets in place down the center. Then topstitch all around the sides and lower edge of the larger pockets, including the lower edges of the small pocket. Topstitch the edge of the triangular pocket to large pocket down lower $\frac{3}{4}$in (2cm) of pocket edges.

12 Insert the cord through casings at waist and wrists, knotting the ends to finish.

Technique tip
Working with stretch terrycloth
Before cutting out, leave the fabric flat on the floor or table overnight to allow it to "relax".
The crosswise edges tend to roll up, as there is more stretch in this direction. To flatten them, pin them to tissue paper. When cutting out, use a "with nap" layout. The pile is especially noticeable on velvety terrycloth.
Use synthetic thread. A shallow zig-zag stitch is preferable but if you have a straight-stitch machine, stretch the seam slightly when sewing it. To finish the seams, unless otherwise instructed, trim seam allowances to $\frac{3}{8}$in (1cm) and finish the two edges by sewing them together with zig-zag stitch.
Use seam binding on seams that are likely to stretch such as shoulders or necklines (see Volume 4, page 61).

SEWING

This zipped sleeping bag is made in cuddly fur fabric with a cheery clown motif. It will keep baby warm at night, and can easily be adapted to make a bathrobe for a toddler.

Sleeping easy

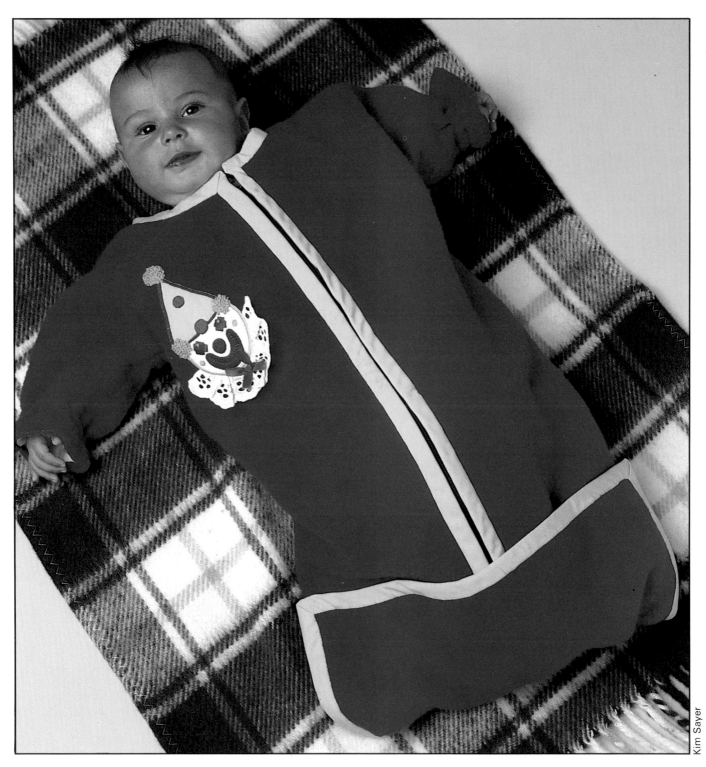

Kim Sayer

Measurements

To fit from 9 months up.
Length from shoulder seam to lower fold, 22in (55.5cm).

Note: As the baby grows remove the snaps from sleeping bag, cut off bottom flap and bind back edge to match front.

Suggested fabrics

Synthetic fur fabric or fleece, ready-quilted cotton. Lining and binding: wool/cotton blends, lightweight synthetic/cotton blends.

Materials

- $\frac{7}{8}$yd (.8m) of 50/54in (125/140cm)-wide fabric or
  $1\frac{1}{4}$yd (1.1m) of 36in (90cm)-wide fabric
- $1\frac{1}{4}$yd (1.1m) of 36in (90cm)-wide lining fabric
- $\frac{5}{8}$yd (.5m) of 36in (90cm)-wide fabric for binding
- Matching thread, eight snaps
- $\frac{5}{8}$yd (.5m) elastic
- 22in (56cm) open-ended zipper
- Appliqué motif or scraps of fabric to use for appliqué
- Flexible curve, yardstick, tailor's chalk

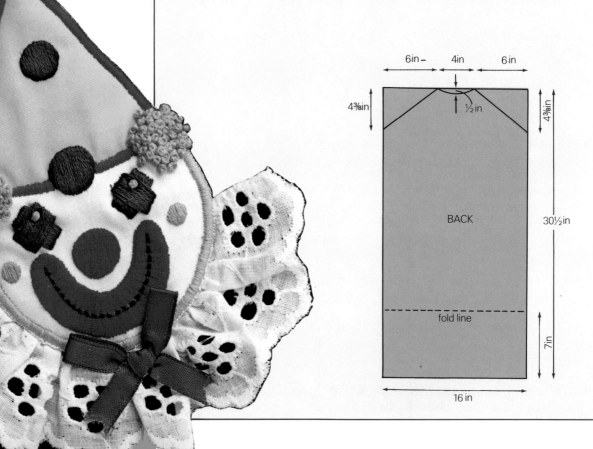

1 Place the fabric on table or cutting board, right side down. Mark one back section, two fronts and two sleeves, following the measurement diagram and cutting layout. (See Technique Tip for directions on cutting out fur fabric.) Cut out the lining, and cut bias strips for binding to make a total length of $3\frac{1}{8}$yd (2.8m). $\frac{5}{8}$in (1.5cm) seam allowances have been included in all pieces. On the back section, mark the foldline with a line of basting.

2 Trace the pieces for the clown's head from the photograph below. Cut out pieces from scraps of fabric in appropriate colors. Pin and baste the pieces to the right front of the sleeping bag, centering them on the piece and positioning them about 6in (15cm) from the top. Set the stitch length to very short zig-zag and stitch in place over the raw edges, or sew by hand using blanket stitch. Eyelet edging makes a realistic ruffle; leave it loose at the lower edges, finishing the ends. Make the hair and pompom with tight French knots and use satin stitch for the features. Add a ribbon bow.

3 With right sides together and raw edges even, pin, baste and stitch sleeves to back and fronts at shoulder seams. Press seams open. (See Technique Tip for directions on sewing and pressing fur fabric.)

4 Fold sleeping bag in half along shoulders, right sides together, matching underarm and side seams. Pin, baste and stitch seams from cuff to underarm and then to hem as far as line of basting on back. Press seams open.

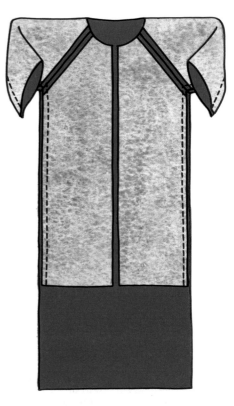

Measurement diagram

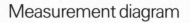

6in — 4in — 6in

$4\frac{3}{8}$in

$\frac{1}{2}$in

$4\frac{3}{8}$in

BACK

$30\frac{1}{2}$in

fold line

7in

16 in

5 Cut out and make lining in the same way and turn right side out.

6 Slip completed lining over the (inside-out) sleeping bag, wrong sides together and seams matching. Pin and baste together around neck and down front edges, keeping raw edges together.

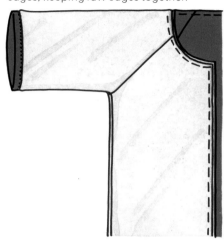

7 At wrist edge, turn in $\frac{5}{8}$in (1.5cm) of outer fabric and $\frac{3}{4}$in (2cm) of lining. Slip stitch together around cuff. Add two lines of stitching around cuff, $\frac{3}{4}$in (2cm) and $1\frac{1}{8}$in (3cm) from finished edge, to form casing for elastic. Make a hole in lining seam and thread elastic through. Cut elastic to fit wrist, allowing $\frac{3}{4}$in (2cm) for joining. Stitch ends securely.

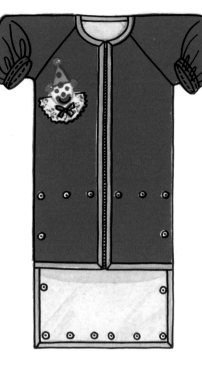

8 Stitch prepared binding all around neck, fronts, front hem and back flap, mitering corners. Insert an open-ended zipper in front opening. Sew six snaps across the lower edge of the bottom flap, on the lined side of the flap. Sew one more on each side of the flap. Sew other half of each snap to front sections to match.

Technique tip
Working with fur fabric

The type of fur fabric suitable for babies' sleeping bags is usually made with a knit backing. This should be stitched with a small zig-zag stitch, as for other knit fabrics.

To cut out, lay the fabric with right side down and mark the pattern pieces on the wrong side. Arrange all the pieces so that the pile runs in the same direction down the length of the garment. Cut only one thickness of fabric at a time.

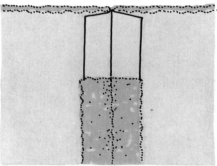

After stitching, shear the pile from the seam allowances, or trim with small scissors.

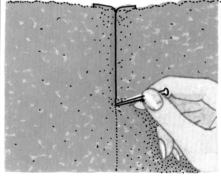

On the right side, lift out the pile that has been caught into the seam, using a pin.

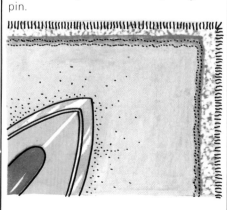

Press fabric on the wrong side, using a velvet board or towel to prevent flattening.

Terry Evans

Cutting layout for 50in/54in-wide fabric

36in-wide fabric

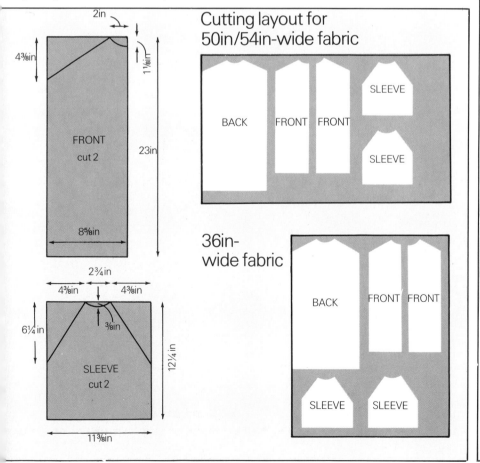

SEWING

Simply sweet

Set aside just one evening to make this charming sundress. It can be worn by itself or with a T-shirt underneath on cooler days. The top is shaped by two rows of elastic threaded through casings, so that the width can be adjusted for a perfect fit.

Measurements
To fit ages 2 to 3, 6 to 7 and 9 to 10.
Finished length: $14\frac{1}{2}[21\frac{5}{8}:25\frac{1}{2}]$in (37[55:65]cm).

Note $\frac{5}{8}$in (1.5cm)-wide seam allowances and 3in (8cm)-wide hem allowances have been included.
Directions for larger sizes are in brackets []; where only one figure is given, this applies to all sizes.

Materials
$1\frac{1}{8}[1\frac{1}{2}:1\frac{3}{4}]$yd $(1[1.3:1.5]m)$ of 36in (90cm)-wide fabric
$2\frac{7}{8}[3\frac{1}{8}:3\frac{1}{2}]$yd $(2.6[2.8:3.2]m)$ of $\frac{1}{2}$in (1.2cm)-wide cotton seam binding for casing
$2\frac{1}{8}$yd (2m) narrow elastic
Matching thread
Scraps of contrasting material for pocket (optional)
Green embroidery floss in two shades (optional)
Embroidery hoop (optional)

Bright-colored material will make this sundress something special. Here we show it made in three different sizes and three different fabrics. We chose yellow gingham, a floral print and a bright apple green for the smallest size. The smallest size is decorated with a bright red apple which is a patch pocket. You will find the directions for making the pocket in the Technique Tip on page 106. For simpler pockets, make plain rectangular patch pockets in a contrasting fabric and topstitch them in place.

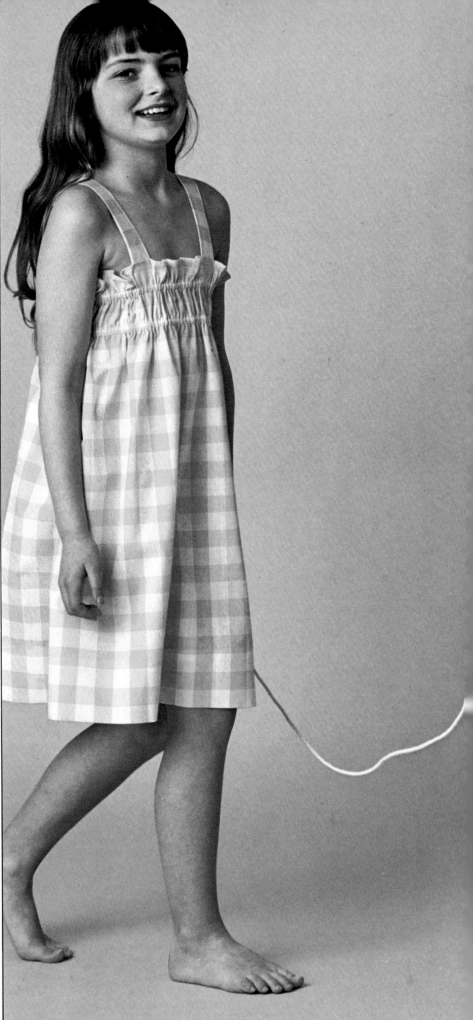

Victor Yuan

Measurement diagram

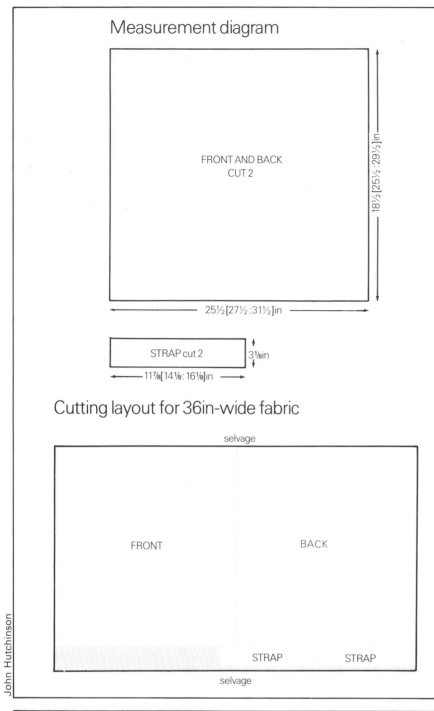

FRONT AND BACK
CUT 2

18½[25½:29½]in

25½[27½:31½]in

STRAP cut 2

3⅛in

11⅞[14⅛:16⅛]in

Cutting layout for 36in-wide fabric

selvage

FRONT

BACK

STRAP

STRAP

selvage

John Hutchinson

1 Cut two body pieces and two straps following the cutting layout and measurement diagram for the size you want.

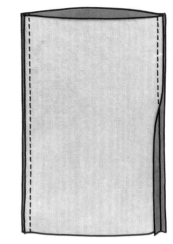

2 With right sides facing, pin, baste and stitch the front and back pieces together down the long edges. Remove basting and press seams open.

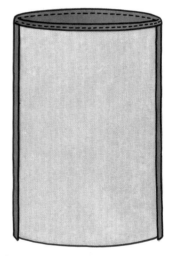

3 To finish top edge of dress, pin and baste a ⅜in (1cm)-wide double hem. Stitch, remove basting and press.

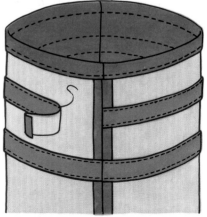

4 Cut two pieces of seam binding, each 1½[1⅝:1¾]yd (1.3[1.4:1.6]m) long.

John Hutchinson

(This includes seam allowances at each end.) Starting at one side seam, ¾in (2cm) below finished edge, pin one piece of binding to wrong side. Turn under raw ends of binding where they meet. Baste and stitch close to both edges of binding. Baste a second row of binding 1⅛in (3cm) below first.

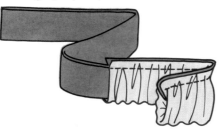

5 Right sides together, fold one strap in half lengthwise. Baste and stitch long edge. Press seam open, then turn strap right side out and press so that the seamline lies in the center. Repeat for the second strap.

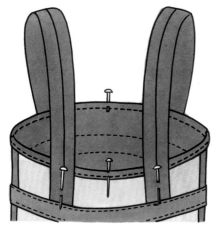

6 Fold dress in half and mark center of top edges, front and back, with pins. Pin shoulder straps in place 3½in (9cm) each side of center back and front.

7 Cut elastic into two pieces. Using a yarn needle or a safety pin; thread one piece of elastic through each casing. Draw up elastic to child's chest measurement and knot temporarily.

8 Try dress on child. Adjust elastic and check length and position of straps. Mark the hemline with pins or tailor's chalk.

9 Turn in ends of straps and slip stitch to finish.

Sew straps onto dress in correct positions. Trim off excess elastic and overcast ends together securely.
Fold up ⅜in (1cm) along hem edge, and stitch.
Turn up again to the depth required and hand-hem. Press.
10 Cut out and make pocket, and embroider leaf and stalk as shown in the Technique Tip (overleaf) if you wish

Victor Yuan

Terry Evans

Victor Yuan

John Hutchinson

Technique tip

Motif patch pocket

The pocket on the green dress is made in the shape of an apple. This is a simple shape, but you can use this method to embroider an animal, another type of fruit or any other design you choose by following the same basic method.

Trace the shape for the apple from the photograph outline above. Transfer the shape to a double thickness of red fabric and add a $\frac{3}{8}$in (1cm) seam allowance all around.

Cut out two red apples.

Pin, baste and stitch together, right sides facing, stitching $\frac{3}{8}$in (1cm) from raw

edges leaving a $1\frac{1}{4}$in (3cm) opening along the lower edge. Trim seam and clip and notch as necessary. Turn it right side out and press, turning in raw edges to make a neatly finished patch pocket.

Pin, baste and stitch motif to dress, positioning it below the right-hand strap,

about half way between the upper and lower edges. Run a double line of topstitching close to the edge, enclosing raw edges of opening along lower edge and leaving a 2in (5cm) opening at top.

Trace the leaf from the photograph and transfer the marking to the dress, placing it as shown below.

Embroider the leaves in any filling stitch you prefer, using pale green floss, and embroider the outlines in stem stitch, using a darker green.

Homemaker

The romantic look

Spike Powell

These exquisite lace-trimmed pillows are ideal for a romantic bedroom.

Pillow with square trimming

Size Pillow measures 16in (41cm) square.

Materials

$\frac{5}{8}$yd (.5m) of 36in (90cm)-wide white fabric, such as linen

8$\frac{1}{2}$in (22cm) square of pale pink fabric

8$\frac{1}{2}$in (22cm) square of white lace fabric

1$\frac{7}{8}$yd (1.7m) of $\frac{3}{8}$in (1cm)-wide pale pink ribbon

$\frac{3}{4}$yd (.7m) of $\frac{3}{4}$in (2cm)-wide white edging lace

1$\frac{1}{4}$yd (1.1m) of 1$\frac{1}{4}$in (3cm)-wide eyelet lace

Scrap of white polka-dot cotton fabric

16in (41cm) square pillow form

1 From white fabric cut out two pieces, each 17$\frac{1}{4}$in (44cm) square.

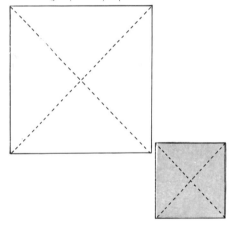

2 Mark the center of the plain white square by folding the fabric diagonally in half twice, as shown. Mark the center of the pink fabric square in the same way.

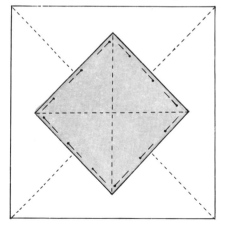

3 Place the pink square, right side up, diagonally over the right side of the white square, matching center points. Pin in place around edges.

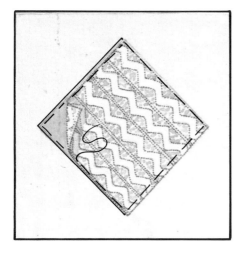

4 Center the white lace square over the pink square and baste in place through all three layers.

5 Pin and baste the eyelet lace, right side up, around the edge of the lace-covered square, just overlapping the fabric edges, mitering the corners. Turn in the ends at one corner and slip stitch them together.

6 Pin and baste the pink ribbon along all sides of the lace-covered square, overlapping the edge of the eyelet lace. Miter the corners and turn in the ends as on the eyelet lace. Topstitch or zig-zag stitch along both edges.

7 Cut the polka dot fabric into four right-angled triangles with two equal sides of 6in (15cm). Place each triangle, right side up, over each corner of pillow front. Pin and baste in place.

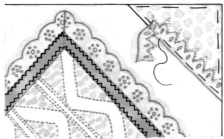

8 Cut the edging lace into four equal pieces. Baste each piece, right side up, along the long edge of each corner triangle, with plain edge inward. Pin and baste a piece of pink ribbon over the edge of the lace at each corner. Topstitch or zig-zag stitch along both edges of ribbon, catching in edges of fabric and lace.
9 Place trimmed square and plain back square together, right sides facing. Pin, baste and stitch around the edges, taking $\frac{5}{8}$in (1.5cm) seams and leaving an opening about 10in (25cm) long in one side.
10 Trim seam allowances and cut diagonally across each corner. Turn pillow cover right side out.
11 Insert pillow form. Turn in the remaining raw edges and slip stitch them together.

Pillow with lace motifs

Size The pillow measures 15in (38cm) square.
Materials
> $\frac{5}{8}$yd (.5m) of 36in (90cm)-wide pink fabric
> 16in (40cm)-square white lacy napkin
> $1\frac{3}{4}$yd (1.6m) of $\frac{3}{4}$in (2cm)-wide eyelet lace with slits for ribbon
> $1\frac{3}{4}$yd (1.6m) of $\frac{1}{4}$in (6mm)-wide velvet ribbon
> $2\frac{1}{4}$yd (2m) of $\frac{3}{8}$in (1cm)-wide white lace edging
> Lace from which motifs can be cut
> 15in (38cm) square pillow form

1 From pink fabric cut out two pieces, each $16\frac{1}{4}$in (41cm) square.

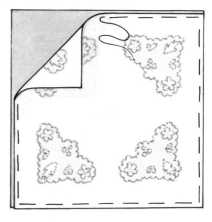

2 Pin and baste the lacy napkin to the right side of one square (the front).

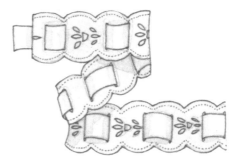

3 Thread the velvet ribbon through the slits in the eyelet lace.

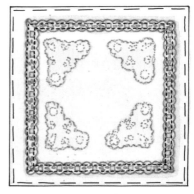

4 Pin and baste the eyelet lace, right side up, all around the pillow front, $1\frac{1}{4}$in (3cm) from the outer edge, mitering each corner. Stitch along both edges.

Terry Evans

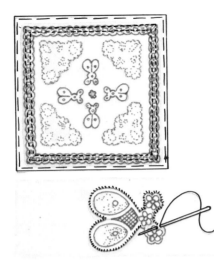

5 Cut out four large motifs and one small one from the piece of lace. Place them in the center of the pillow front, as shown. Pin, baste and sew in place.

6 Pin the lace edging around the four sides of the square, $\frac{3}{8}$in (1cm) from the edge, placing right sides together, so that the finished edge of lace lies inward. Baste in place.

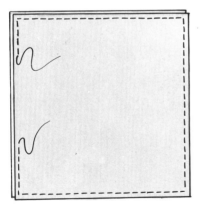

7 Place trimmed front piece and back piece together with right sides facing and raw edges matching. Pin, baste and stitch all around, taking a $\frac{5}{8}$in (1.5cm) seam and leaving an opening about 10in (25cm) long in one side.

8 Trim seam allowances and cut corners diagonally. Turn right side out.

9 Insert pillow form. Turn in remaining raw edges and slip stitch them together.

White oblong pillow

Size The pillow measures 18×14in (45×35cm), excluding lace edging.

Materials

- 19×15in (47.5×37.5cm) lace place mat
- $\frac{5}{8}$yd (.5m) of 36in (90cm)-wide white fabric
- $2\frac{1}{4}$yd (2m) of 1in (2.5cm)-wide gathered eyelet lace
- $2\frac{1}{4}$yd (2m) of $1\frac{3}{4}$in (4.5cm)-wide flat eyelet lace
- 18×14in (45×35cm) pillow form

1 Cut two rectangles each $19\frac{1}{4}×15\frac{1}{4}$in (48×38cm) from white fabric.

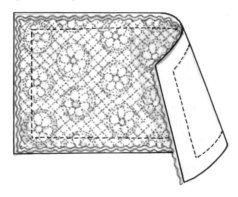

2 Pin and baste place mat, right side up, to right side of one rectangle (the front). Topstitch in place, $1\frac{1}{4}$in (3cm) from the edge of the fabric.

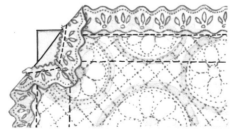

3 Pin, baste and stitch the gathered eyelet lace, right side upward, under the edge of the place mat, as shown, keeping it free from the pillow front fabric and mitering the corners.

4 Pin the $1\frac{3}{4}$in (4.5cm)-wide eyelet lace around the pillow front, $\frac{3}{8}$in (1cm) from the edge, with right sides together and with finished edge of lace lying inward. Baste in place, being careful not to catch in the edge of the place mat.

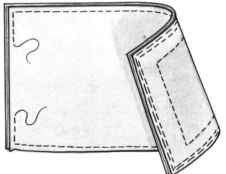

5 Place the front and back rectangles together with right sides facing. Pin, baste and stitch all around, taking a $\frac{5}{8}$in (1.5cm) seam and leaving an opening about 10in (25cm) long in one short side. While basting, be careful to push all the lace edges toward the center so that they will not get caught in the stitching.

6 Trim seams and cut diagonally across each corner. Turn pillow cover right side out.

7 Insert pillow form. Turn in the remaining raw edges and slip stitch them together.

Terry Evans

Homemaker

Bright and beautiful

Gather up some daffodils for a dust ruffle and matching coverlet
that will bring spring to your bedroom.

Materials

For a standard twin bed:
8yd (7.4m) of 55in (140cm)
wide fabric
7yd (6.5m) of 3½in (9cm)
wide eyelet lace edging
2⅜yd (2.1m) of 48in (122cm)
wide drapery lining fabric in white

Note Instructions for calculating the fabric for larger beds are also given.

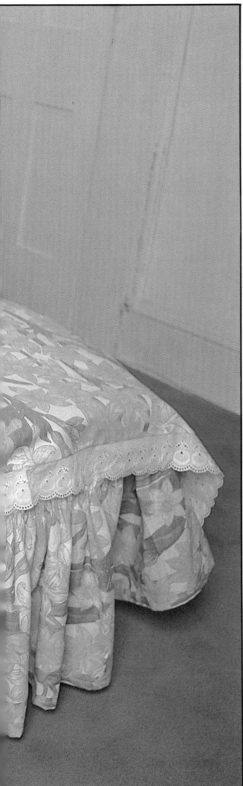

Coverlet

Calculating fabric and joining widths

1 A coverlet used with a dust ruffle should just cover the top of the dust ruffle. To estimate the fabric needed for the coverlet, first measure the length and width of the mattress. Then add twice the depth of the mattress, plus 4in (10cm) to each dimension. Therefore, on a standard twin bed, 78 × 39in (200 × 100cm), you can use 55in (140cm) wide fabric without joining widths. For a double bed, or if you are using a narrower fabric, you will need twice the final length measurement, plus extra for matching patterns.

2 Narrower fabrics will have to be joined by stitching half widths of fabric to a central panel. Cut two pieces of fabric, making sure the pattern matches. Cut one piece in half lengthwise, making two half widths. Cut off the selvages so the fabric will not pucker. Baste the two half widths to each side of the center panel, matching the pattern exactly, and stitch.

3 You will also need enough 3½in (9cm) wide eyelet lace edging for two lengths and one width of the total measurements of the coverlet, plus 10in (25cm) for mitered corners and hems.

Assembling

1 Join the fabric lengthwise in panels, as described above, if necessary.

2 With right sides together, baste the lace to the coverlet, beginning at the lower edge and mitering the corners.

Terry Evans

3 Sew the lace in place. Press seams toward coverlet and finish them with zig-zag stitch or overcasting. Turn under a ⅝in (1.5cm) double hem on top edge of both fabric and lace. Baste and sew by machine or by hand. .
Press the hem.

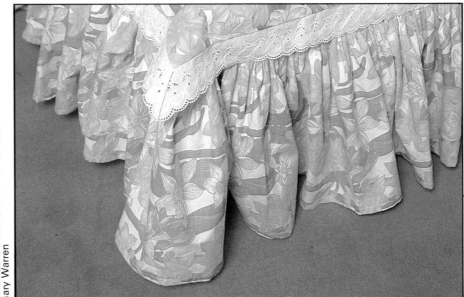

Gary Warren

4 Finish the raw edges of the mitered corners. Finally finish the raw edges of the seam and press the seam allowances toward the coverlet.

Dust ruffle

Calculating the amount of fabric and cutting out

1 For covering the base of the bed, measure the length and width of the bed, without the mattress, and add $\frac{5}{8}$in (1.5cm) all around for seams. For a bed wider than a standard twin size, you may need to double the length measurement and join widths.

2 Cut the drapery lining fabric to the correct proportions (first joining widths if necessary). If the corners of the bed are rounded, mark their shape on the fabric with tailor's chalk and trim away excess fabric, still leaving $\frac{5}{8}$in (1.5cm) seam allowance outside the marked corner line.

3 For the dust ruffle length you will need six times the length of the bed, plus three times the width, plus $1\frac{1}{4}$in (3cm) for each side hem and $1\frac{1}{4}$in (3cm) for each seam. For the ruffle depth, measure the depth of the bed to the floor and add $1\frac{7}{8}$in (4.5cm) for the seam and hem.

4 The sections for the dust ruffle are cut down the length. To calculate how much fabric you will need, divide the width of the fabric you have chosen by the unfinished depth of the dust ruffle. Then

divide the total length of the dust ruffle by the number of strips you can get from each width. For example, if you are using 55in (140cm) wide fabric and your dust ruffle (unfinished) is 17in (43cm) deep, you can cut 3 strips from it. If your total length is $16\frac{1}{4}$yd (15m), divide this length by 3. Thus, you need $5\frac{1}{2}$yd (5m) of fabric for the dust ruffle.

Making the dust ruffle

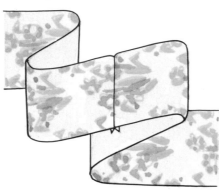

1 Cut the dust ruffle strips to the required size and join all the strips with flat seams, matching the pattern exactly (if it is a large pattern). Finish seams on the wrong side and press them flat.

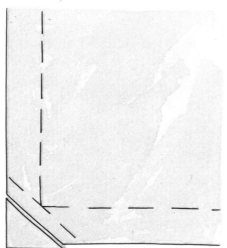

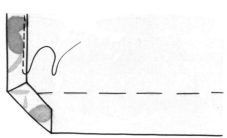

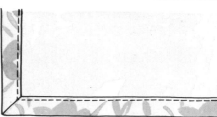

2 Turn under and stitch a $\frac{5}{8}$in (1.5cm)-wide double hem at each end of the dust ruffle and hem along the lower edge, mitering corners as shown below left and above.

3 Turn under and stitch a $\frac{5}{8}$in (1.5cm) double hem at top edge of lining.

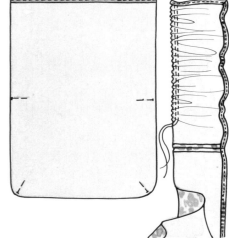

4 Run 2 lines of gathering $\frac{5}{8}$in (1.5cm) from the raw edge all around the upper edge of the dust ruffle; this is easiest to do in five sections—two for each side and one for the bottom. For standard twin beds you can make these sections equal; otherwise, divide the dust ruffle proportionately to the bed dimensions so that the fullness will be equally distributed along the entire length.

5 Mark the center of the long sides and the corners of the lining with pins.

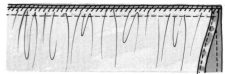

6 Baste and stitch the dust ruffle to the lining with right sides together and matching the ends of each gathered section to the pins as appropriate. Finish the raw edges of the seam and press upward.

Terry Evans

Homemaker

Cutwork elegance

This beautiful cutwork tablecloth is embroidered using a swing-needle sewing machine. Pick solid-color cotton and slightly darker thread for a rich effect.

Geoffrey Frosh

Finished size
59in (150cm) in diameter.

Materials

- 3⅜yd (3m) of 45in (115cm)-wide solid cotton fabric
- Fourteen spools of slightly darker sewing thread
- 8in (20cm)-diameter wooden embroidery hoop
- Tracing paper
- Dressmaker's carbon paper
- 30in (76cm)-square sheet of white paper; sharp scissors

1 Trace the design shown on pages 115-117, matching green broken lines to complete one section of the design.

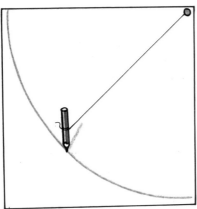

2 On the sheet of white paper draw a quarter circle, using string and a pencil. Tie one end of the string around a thumbtack. Tie the opposite end of string around the pencil, with the string 29½in (75cm) long. Fasten the thumbtack in one corner of the paper. Keeping the string taut, draw an arc from corner to corner. This forms one quarter of the tablecloth pattern.

3 Transfer the traced design twice onto the white paper pattern: transfer the section once, then remove the tracing paper and trace again to complete the quarter, re-aligning the design with the edge of the first section. This forms the pattern for one quarter of the tablecloth.

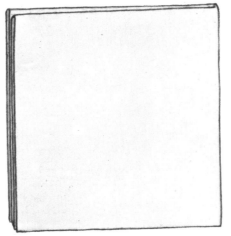

4 Cut the fabric in half widthwise; seam the two halves, then trim the piece to a 59in (150cm) square. Fold the fabric in half and then in half again and finger-crease the foldlines.

5 Open out the fabric and place it on a firm surface. Place the dressmaker's carbon paper and then the white paper pattern over one quarter of the fabric. Match the corner point and straight sides of pattern to center point and foldlines of fabric. Transfer the pattern.

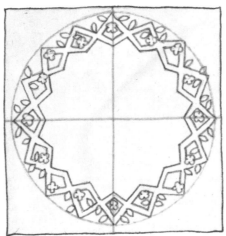

6 Repeat at each quarter to give the complete tablecloth design, adjusting if necessary to fit.

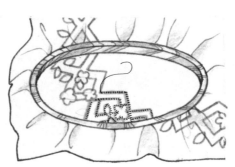

7 Embroider each part of the design with the help of an embroidery hoop. Stretch a section of the fabric to be embroidered in the wooden hoop, so that it lies flat on a working surface, right side up.

8 Set your sewing machine to ⅛in (3mm) zig-zag stitch with the minimum length so that a solid line of satin stitching is produced. Remove the presser foot temporarily and place the embroidery hoop with the area to be stitched on the bed of the machine. Replace the presser foot and lower it to begin stitching.

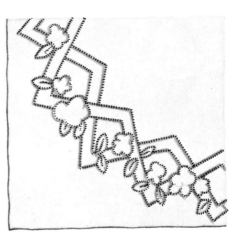

9 Carefully work lines of satin stitch over all the lines of the design. Work the lattice work first, then the leaves, stems and flowers within the area of the hoop.
10 When repositioning the hoop to the next part of the fabric to be worked, remember to remove the presser foot in order to remove the hoop from the machine sewing area.
11 Tie off all the loose threads each time you re-position the hoop.
12 Continue around the tablecloth until all the design has been embroidered.
13 Press the embroidery carefully on the wrong side of the fabric.

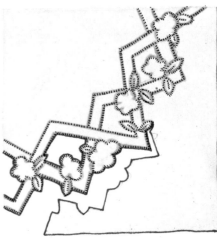

14 Using a pair of sharp-pointed scissors, carefully cut away the excess fabric from around the tablecloth and from within the diamond shapes of the lattice work to form the cutwork edging.
15 Starch and press the wrong side of the tablecloth to make the embroidery more pronounced and to give a firmness to the cutwork flowers and leaves so they will hang well.

Terry Evans

Note: The full-size patterns shown here and overleaf join together to make one-eighth of the tablecloth design. Draw the pattern on tracing paper, matching the green lines to complete the section.

Homemaker

Simple seating

Perfect for a playroom, or for any room where informality is the keynote, these comfortable floor pillows—like giant bean bags—adapt instantly to any position.

Materials
- $3\frac{7}{8}$yd (3.5m) of 48in (122cm)-wide
  patterned fabric
- $3\frac{7}{8}$yd (3.5m) of 48in (122cm)-wide
  lining
- 16 cubic feet (.43 cubic meters) of
  polystyrene beads
- Matching thread

Note A seam allowance of $\frac{1}{2}$in (1.3cm) is
included throughout.

Kim Sayer

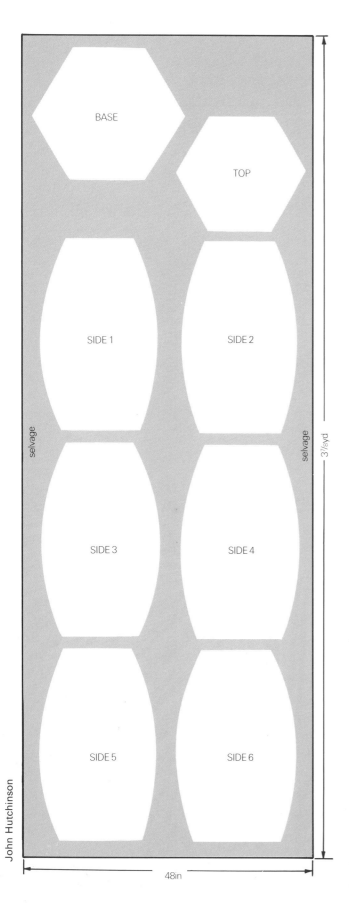

BASE

TOP

SIDE 1

SIDE 2

SIDE 3

SIDE 4

SIDE 5

SIDE 6

selvage

selvage

3⅞yd

48in

John Hutchinson

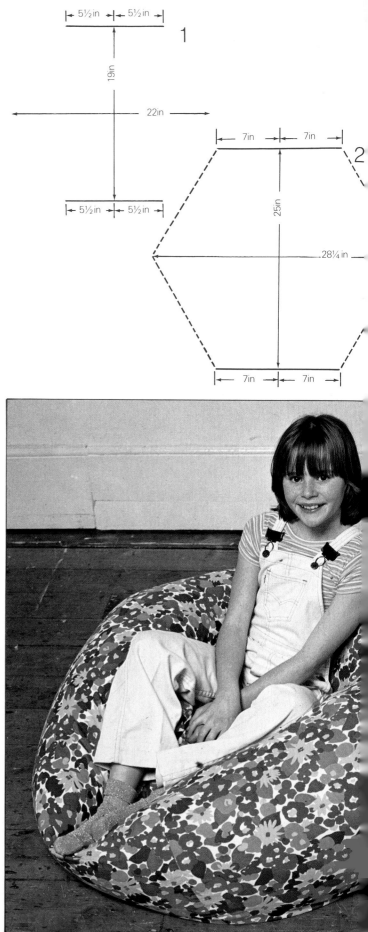

5½ in — 5½ in

19in

22in

1

5½ in — 5½ in

7in — 7in

2

25in

28¼ in

7in — 7in

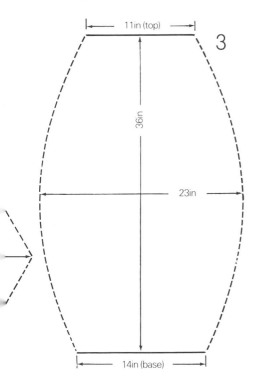

11in (top)

3

36in

23in

14in (base)

1 Make a paper pattern for the top. Draw a vertical line 19in (48cm) long. Draw a horizontal line through the center of vertical line, 22in (56cm) long. At each end of vertical line draw horizontal lines, parallel to center line, each 11in (28cm) long. Join the ends of the long horizontal line to the ends of the short horizontal lines.
2 Make a paper pattern for base, in the same way, but make main vertical line 25in (64cm) long, main horizontal line 28¼in (72cm) long and horizontal lines at each end 14in (36cm) long.
3 Make pattern for side section. Draw a vertical line 36in (90cm) long. Draw a horizontal line through the center 23in (58.5cm) long. At one end draw a horizontal line 11in (28cm) long for the top and at opposite end draw a horizontal line 14in (36cm) long for the base. Join the outer points of top and base, drawing freehand through outer point on center line to make a curved shape. Repeat on opposite side.
4 From patterned fabric cut one top, one base and six side sections.
5 Place two side sections together, right

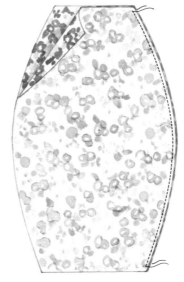

sides facing. Pin, baste and sew along one side edge to within ½in (1.3cm) of each end.

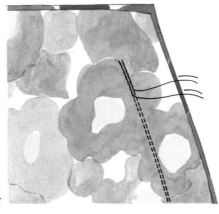

6 Sew down seam again, inside the

seam allowance and close to the first line of stitching, for added strength.
7 Repeat, sewing all the side sections together in the same way to form a tube.

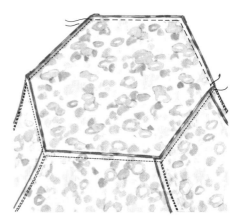

8 Leave the bag wrong side out. Place the top section, wrong side up, over the smaller opening, and pin it in place, matching raw edges—right sides facing—and aligning side seams with corner points. Stitch seam twice, as before.
9 Sew base in place in the same way, but leave two sides open. Turn bag right side out.
10 Make the lining the same way but leave only one side open.
11 Using a saucepan or bowl as a scoop, fill the lining with beads. The beads will not fill the bag completely; this allows room for them to move when someone sits on the cushion.
12 Turn in opening edges of lining and overcast them together firmly. Use button thread for extra strength.

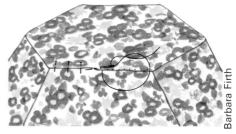

Barbara Firth

13 Push filled lining inside outer cover. Turn under opening edges and slip stitch them together firmly.

Note We chose heavy cotton for our cushions, but they can be made in a variety of fabrics, including thick knits, woolens, corduroy or synthetic leather or suede. To make them even more colorful you can alternate the colors of the sides, top and base—this is also a good way to use up left-over remnants of fabric. The top and bottom sections together take less than 1yd (90cm) of fabric.

It is possible to cut two side pieces from 1yd (90cm) of fabric.

Kim Sayer

Clowning around

The circus comes to town in this child's mobile. It's made in bright colors and trimmed with stitching and sequins.

Materials

Two 8½in (22cm) squares of pink felt
8½in (22cm) squares of felt in mauve, yellow, blue, green and dark pink
Scraps of black and white felt
Stranded embroidery floss in blue, pale green, yellow, cerise and black
Silver yarn
Two pipecleaners
One pack of mixed sequins
Three pompoms in red and three in yellow cut from pompom fringe
Piece of red and white ribbon 10in (25cm) long
Suitable stuffing
Fabric glue
Tracing paper and pencil
Two wooden dowel sticks
Crochet cotton in green

Note The front and back of each clown are decorated separately and then they are sewn together.

Bonzo

1 Using tracing paper and a sharp pencil trace the front and back patterns from page 124. Cut out both patterns.

2 Cut out one complete front and one complete back in pink felt.

3 Cut up the tracing paper patterns into individual pieces—the coat, coat lapels, pants, hair and handkerchief from the front pattern; the coat, coat collar, pants and hair from the back pattern.

4 Cut out the clothes and hair in felt following the diagrams for the appropriate colors.

5 Using fabric glue, apply the blue coat and lapels, green pants, yellow hair and dark pink handkerchief neatly to the complete pink felt front.

6 Now glue the clown's coat, collar, pants and hair in place on the complete pink felt back.

7 Sew a large white sequin to coat front, positioning it to one side, at the base of the coat lapel as if it were a button.

8 Sew six small white sequins to decorate the handkerchief on the coat front.

9 Sew 13 small green sequins all over the coat lapels to decorate both of them.

10 For features, following diagram on page 124 for shapes, cut out eyebrows in yellow felt. Cut out nose and mouth in dark pink felt.

Jean Paul Frogett

11 Following diagram for positions, glue mouth, nose and eyebrows to front of face. For the eyes, make two French knots in blue embroidery floss underneath the eyebrows.

pipecleaner for hooked end. Cut a $\frac{1}{4}$in (5mm)-wide strip of yellow felt about 12in (·30cm) long. Wind and glue the yellow felt strip around the cane at a diagonal angle. Pin the cane to the wrong side of the front of the right hand.

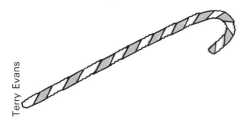

Terry Evans

12 For cane cut a 5in (13cm) piece of pipecleaner. Bend over one end of

13 Place front and back bodies together, wrong sides facing, matching outer edges. Pin and baste together. Using three strands of blue embroidery floss, overcast the front and back pieces together, catching the cane between the right hands and filling the clown with a small amount of stuffing as you sew to give the clown a slightly rounded shape. *(continued page 128)*

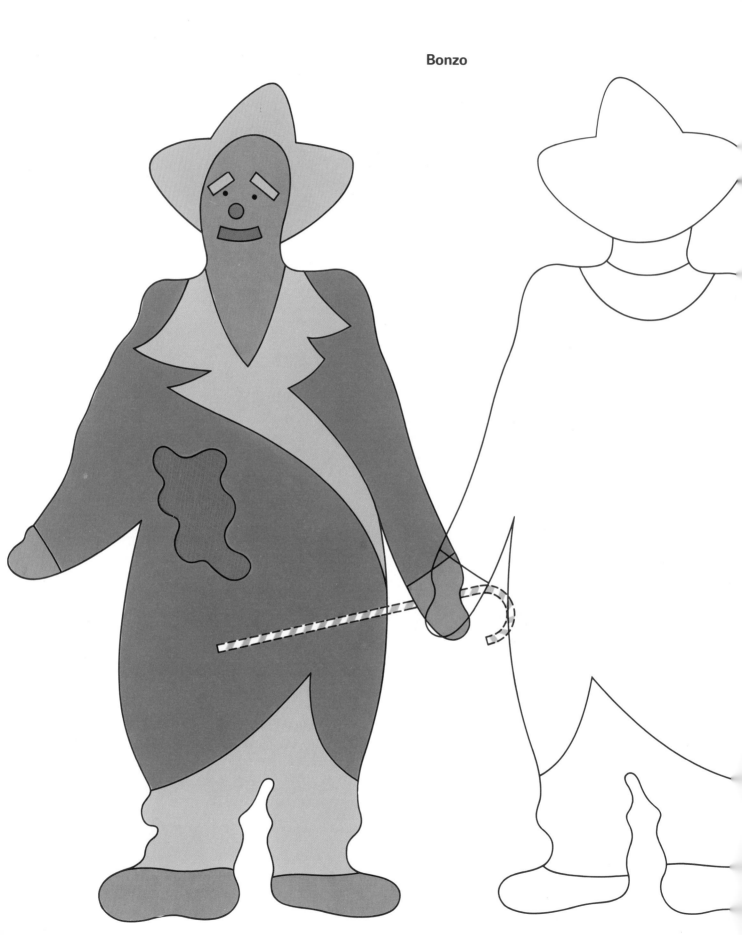

Bimbo

Pogo

1 Trace patterns as for Bonzo, step 1.
2 Cut out one complete front and one complete back in mauve felt.
3 Cut the tracing paper patterns into individual pieces—the face, trumpet, hands and socks from the front pattern, the hair, neck and socks from the back pattern.
4 Cut out the clothes and hair in felt following the diagrams for the appropriate colors.
5 Using fabric glue, apply the face, trumpet, hands and socks in place on the complete mauve felt front.
6 Now glue the hair, neck and socks in place on the complete mauve felt back.
7 Using cerise embroidery floss, outline the arms on front body in stem stitch. Make straight stitches in the same thread over the edge of both wrists.
8 For features, following diagrams for shapes, cut out cheeks in dark pink felt. Following diagrams for positions, glue cheeks to front of face. Using cerise embroidery floss, work two French knots for nostrils. Using black embroidery floss, work eyes in French knots and eyebrows in stem stitch.
9 Sew front and back bodies together as for Bonzo, step 13, omitting cane and using cerise embroidery floss.
10 Sew one red pompom to hat point and one red pompom to top of each shoe.

Bimbo

1 Trace patterns and cut out in pink felt as for Bonzo, steps 1 and 2.
2 Cut the tracing paper patterns into individual pieces—the face, pants with suspenders, boots, patches and hair from the front pattern; the pants with suspenders, boots, patches and hair from the back pattern.
3 Cut out the clothes and hair in felt, following the diagrams for the appropriate colors.
4 Using fabric glue, apply the face, hair, pants, patches and boots to the complete pink felt front.

5 Now glue the clown's hair, pants, patches and boots in place on the complete pink felt back.
6 Overcast the patches to the front and back pants using contrasting embroidery floss. Sew small sequins in matching colors to the patches on pants front only.
7 Cut 28 strips of blue felt, each $\frac{1}{8}$ x $\frac{3}{8}$in (3mm x 1cm). Glue seven in place down the length of the suspenders on both front and back pants.
8 Sew small sequins to pants front at base of each strap for buttons.
9 For features, following diagrams for shapes, cut out the eyebrows in mauve felt, the eyes in blue felt and the nose and mouth in dark pink felt.
10 Following diagrams for positions, glue features to the face.
11 Sew front and back bodies together as for Bonzo, step 13, omitting cane and using green embroidery floss.
12 Sew a yellow pompom to each hand.

Zeppo

1 Trace patterns as for Bonzo, step 1.
2 Cut out one complete front and one complete back in yellow felt.
3 Cut up the tracing paper patterns into individual pieces—the hat, hat band, face and neck, vest, coat lapels, coat, boots and boot tips from the front pattern; the hat, hat band, back head, collar, coat, boots and boot tips from the back pattern.
4 Cut out the clothes and face in felt, following the diagrams for the appropriate colors.
5 Decorate the pants part of both back and front. Pin lengths of silver yarn over front to form $\frac{3}{4}$in (2cm) squares. Make a diagonal stitch over each intersection in cerise embroidery floss. Repeat for back.
6 Use cerise embroidery floss to outline the pants legs on front. Work the outline in stem stitch.
7 Now glue the clown's hat, hat band, face, vest, lapels, coat, boots and boot tips in place on the complete yellow felt front.

8 Glue the hat, hat band, back head, collar, coat, boots and boot tips in place on the complete yellow felt back.
9 Outline the sleeves on front and back, and pocket on front of pants. Use cerise embroidery floss and work in stem stitch.
10 Make eight French knots down the center of the vest front in yellow embroidery floss.
11 Embroider straight stitches in yellow embroidery floss on boot fronts and backs for laces.
12 Cut a 4in (10cm) piece of pipecleaner for flower stem. From yellow felt cut out two flower heads. From pink felt cut out two flower centers. Glue flower centers to flower heads. Glue the flower heads together, inserting one end of pipecleaner stem in between. Pin other end of stem behind hat front on the left-hand side.
13 For features, following diagrams for shapes, cut out outer eyes in blue felt. Cut out pupils in black felt. Cut out nose in dark pink felt. Cut out mouth in pink felt.
14 Following diagram for positions, glue eyes, nose and mouth in place on face.
15 Sew front and back bodies together as for Bonzo, step 13, omitting cane, but catching flower on hat and working in yellow embroidery floss.
16 Tie red and white ribbon in a bow. Sew bow to neck front.

To assemble mobile

1 Make a notch in the center of one dowel stick.
2 Place the second stick across the first with centers matching. Glue together.
3 Thread a length of crochet cotton about 8in (20cm) long through the top of each clown.
4 For Bimbo, thread yellow pompom onto hanging thread, 2in (5cm) from his head.
5 Tie the other end of the thread around the ends of each stick. Adjust the length of the thread, so the clowns hang at different heights. To adjust the balance move the threads nearer the center. When the clowns hang correctly, notch the sticks where the threads are fastened.

Jean Paul Frogget